# The 1960s

JENNIFER A. HURLEY

Greenhaven Press, Inc., San Diego, California

Library of Congress Cataloging-in-Publication Data

Hurley, Jennifer A., 1973–
      The 1960s / Jennifer A. Hurley.
          p.     cm. — (Opposing viewpoints digests)
      Includes bibliographical references and index.
      Summary: Presents opposing viewpoints on events of the 1960s including the Vietnam War, social rebellion, the civil rights movement, and the women's liberation movement.
      ISBN 0-7377-0211-7 (lib. : alk. paper). — ISBN 0-7377-0210-9 (pbk. : alk. paper)
      1. United States—Social conditions—1960–1980—Juvenile literature. 2. Political culture—United States—History—20th century—Juvenile literature. 3. Nineteen sixties—Juvenile literature. 4. Youth—United States—Political activity—History—20th century—Juvenile literature. [1. United States—Social conditions—1960–1980. 2. Nineteen sixties] I. Title. II. Series.
HN59.H87  2000
306'.0973—dc21                                                          99-38546
                                                                                CIP

Cover Photo: Corbis/Bettman
AP/Wide World: 17, 51
Corbis/Bettman: 40
LBJ Library: 65
Library of Congress: 7, 78
National Archives: 23
UPI Corbis Bettman: 34

©2000 by Greenhaven Press, Inc.
PO Box 289009, San Diego, CA 92198-9009
Printed in the U.S.A.

# CONTENTS

# FOREWORD

*The only way in which a human being can make some approach to knowing the whole of a subject is by hearing what can be said about it by persons of every variety of opinion and studying all modes in which it can be looked at by every character of mind. No wise man ever acquired his wisdom in any mode but this.*

—John Stuart Mill

Greenhaven Press's Opposing Viewpoints Digests in history are designed to aid in examining important historical issues in a way that develops critical thinking and evaluating skills. Each book presents thought-provoking argument and stimulating debate on a single topic. In analyzing issues through opposing views, students gain a social and historical context that cannot be discovered in textbooks. Excerpts from primary sources reveal the personal, political, and economic side of historical topics such as the American Revolution, the Great Depression, and the Bill of Rights. Students begin to understand that history is not a dry recounting of facts, but a record founded on ideas—ideas that become manifest through lively discussion and debate. Digests immerse students in contemporary discussions: Why did many colonists oppose a bill of rights? What was the original intent of the New Deal and on what grounds was it criticized? These arguments provide a foundation for students to assess today's debates on censorship, welfare, and other issues. For example, *The Great Depression: Opposing Viewpoints Digests* offers opposing arguments on controversial issues of the time as well as views and interpretations that interest modern historians. A major debate during Franklin D. Roosevelt's administration was whether the president's New Deal programs would lead to a permanent welfare state, creating a citizenry dependent on government money. *The Great Depression* covers this issue from both historical and modern perspectives, allowing students to critically evaluate arguments both in the context of their time and through the benefit of historical hindsight.

This emphasis on debate makes Digests a useful tool for writing reports, research papers, and persuasive essays. In addition to supplying students with a range of possible topics and supporting material, the Opposing Viewpoints Digests offer unique features through which young readers acquire and sharpen critical thinking and reading skills. To assure an appropriate and consistent reading level for young adults, all essays in each volume are written by a single author. Each essay heavily quotes readable primary sources that are fully cited to allow for further research and documentation. Thus, primary sources are introduced in a context to enhance comprehension.

In addition, each volume includes extensive research tools, including a section comprising excerpts from original documents pertaining to the issue under discussion. In *The Bill of Rights*, for example, readers can examine the English Magna Carta, the Virginia State Bill of Rights drawn up in 1776, and various opinions by U.S. Supreme Court justices in key civil rights cases, as well as an unabridged version of the U.S. Bill of Rights. These documents both complement the text and give students access to a wide variety of relevant sources in a single volume. Additionally, a "facts about" section allows students to peruse facts and statistics that pertain to the topic. These statistics are also fully cited, allowing students to question and analyze the credibility of the source. Two bibliographies, one for young adults and one listing the author's sources, are also included; both are annotated to guide student research. Finally, a comprehensive index allows students to scan and locate content efficiently.

Greenhaven's Opposing Viewpoints Digests, like Greenhaven's higher level and critically acclaimed Opposing Viewpoints Series, have been developed around the concept that an awareness and appreciation for the complexity of seemingly simple issues is particularly important in a democratic society. In a democracy, the common good is often, and very appropriately, decided by open debate of widely varying views. As one of democracy's greatest advocates, Thomas Jefferson, observed, "Difference of opinion leads to inquiry, and inquiry to truth." It is to this principle that Opposing Viewpoints Digests are dedicated.

# A Historical Overview of Sixties' Activism

The first instance of sixties' activism occurred, as though on cue, on February 1, 1960. On this date, four black students from Agricultural and Technical College in Greensboro, North Carolina, sat down at the local Woolworth's lunch counter, which at the time was only open to whites, and requested coffee. Although the white waitress refused to serve them, the students stayed seated at the counter, amid taunts and police intimidation, until the store closed that evening.

The following morning, the Greensboro Four, as they were called by the press, arrived at the Woolworth's lunch counter along with twenty-five other black men and women. They were joined the next day by an even larger group, which included three white students from Greensboro College. By the end of the week, the sit-in at Woolworth's had drawn hundreds of students, and similar protests were spreading throughout the community. As Franklin McCain, one of the Greensboro Four, said, "It spread to places like the shopping centers, the drugstores in the shopping centers, the drive-ins. No place was going to be left untouched. . . . If it did not serve blacks, it was certainly going to be hit."[1]

Many whites in Greensboro reacted first with shock, then with violence. Local white youths harassed and assaulted the demonstrators. Someone telephoned Woolworth's and threatened to detonate a bomb if the sit-in continued. For the protesters, the important thing was that the public had taken notice. Although sit-ins had been taking place throughout the South for years, these had been ignored for the most part. The Greensboro sit-in, in contrast, gained the attention of public officials and spurred hundreds of other sit-ins throughout the South. In the month following the event, activists were using the tactic in seven states and more than thirty communities, ranging from Chattanooga to Baltimore. Soon, even small towns such as Xenia, Ohio, were the sites of civil rights sit-ins.

In essence, the Greensboro Four touched off an entire movement that would eventually involve thousands of Americans, both black and white, in the struggle for racial equality. Although the civil rights movement had powerful and articulate leaders, the most famous of whom was Reverend Martin Luther King Jr., it was primarily a grassroots movement. Black Americans, inspired by early civil rights suc-

*The Greensboro Four stage a sit-in at a Woolworth's lunch counter that refused to serve black customers.*

cesses, but still deeply frustrated by the innumerable laws and conventions that limited their freedoms and by the violence they sometimes suffered at the hands of whites, began to work actively for change. They did this through civil disobedience—the nonviolent refusal to obey unjust laws. This form of protest was soon adopted by other activist movements.

## The Seeds of Social Revolt

The revolt of black youth against racial segregation inspired other groups to challenge the status quo—specifically, the cold war culture of the fifties. During the 1950s, the fear of a nuclear attack by the communist Soviet Union incited widespread paranoia of communism. The U.S. government, led by Senator Joseph McCarthy, took extraordinary measures to expose suspected spies and traitors. Political speech was curtailed, and citizens in position of influence—such as politicians or university professors—were interrogated by Congress about their views on communism. While some people saw these activities as necessary means to protect national security, others viewed them as a horrific abuse of government power. According to writers Alexander Bloom and Wini Breines, "Civil liberties were constricted, thousands lost their jobs, books were banned, passports lifted—all rationalized under the rubric of the domestic fight against communism."[2]

These government "witch-hunts" to expose communists, along with the threat of nuclear war itself, created a society in which security was people's principal concern. Therefore, the fifties' culture embraced the stable, homogeneous suburban life with its simple rules and expectations. No one wanted to be perceived as "different." Dubbed the Silent Generation, the generation of the fifties "didn't challenge any authority, take any risks, or ask any questions . . . they were bereft of passions, of dreams, of gods."[3]

Many of the children of this generation, however, felt that the fifties' image of the happy American family was a façade that concealed disturbing truths about society. In a manifesto adopted at a 1962 meeting at Port Huron, Michigan, the Students for a Democratic Society (SDS) began to question the nation's values:

> We are people of this generation, bred in at least modest comfort, housed now in universities, looking uncomfortably to the world we inherit . . . . As we grew . . . our comfort was penetrated by events too troubling to dismiss. First, the permeating and victimizing fact of human degradation, symbolized by the Southern struggle against racial bigotry, compelled most of us from silence to activism. Second, the enclosing fact of the Cold War, symbolized by the presence of the Bomb, brought awareness that we ourselves, and millions of abstract "others" . . . might die at any time.[4]

The SDS manifesto marked the public emergence of the New Left, a political student movement that challenged various aspects of society such as the societal inequalities of race and class, the materialism inspired by capitalism, and the U.S. development of nuclear weapons. Later in the decade, its activities would center around protesting the Vietnam War.

The student movement had many abstract political goals, but many of its actions focused on eradicating restrictions on free speech. In 1964, the Free Speech Movement of the University of California at Berkeley worked to overturn a ban on political speech on campus—a ban that had aimed to prevent students from expressing opinions that were critical of the government.

## Optimism and Disillusionment

During the early sixties, activists challenged the American "system," and for the most part, were confident that this system could—and would—be changed for the better. President John F. Kennedy's firm commitment to racial equality inspired hope among civil rights activists, whose protests were met with brutal violence by racist communities and police in the South. This spirit of hope was made vivid by the scores of civil rights protesters who sang "We Shall Overcome" from within southern jails. As former SDS leader Todd Gitlin contends, 1963 was a time when "the democratic promise came alive, the arms race, racism, and poverty seemed solvable problems, and the New Left looked as though it might push liberalism beyond its old limits. . . . That whole year was full of signs of opening."[5]

One of the people most associated with the country's optimism was President John F. Kennedy. Young, charismatic, and passionate about the subject of social justice, Kennedy seemed to stand for all that was good about America. Although he faced criticism from some civil rights leaders, who felt he was too slow in acting on civil rights legislation, Kennedy was an enormously popular leader—especially with African Americans and young people.

However, on November 22, 1963, the country's utopian spirit came to an abrupt end. While waving to crowds from a convertible in Dallas, Texas, Kennedy was shot in the head and killed, an event that horrified the nation. Americans reacted to the news of Kennedy's assassination with an outpouring of grief. Public schools and some businesses were closed, and people held a mournful vigil around televisions to watch the news coverage of the assassination. On November 24, millions of viewers, watching Kennedy's alleged assassin Lee Harvey Oswald being transferred from his Dallas jail cell, witnessed Jack Ruby emerge from a crowd and shoot Oswald. The death of Oswald fueled a variety of conspiracy theories about the assassination—theories that contributed to the widespread feelings of confusion and disillusionment resulting from Kennedy's sudden death.

For many black Americans, the assassination of Kennedy, combined with their growing realization that civil rights legislation did not necessarily mean equality, extinguished their hope for change. Although President Lyndon B. Johnson, Kennedy's successor, passed laws banning racial segregation and other forms of discrimination, many black Americans did not see the impact of such laws in their daily lives. On August 11, 1965, just days after Johnson passed an act intended to guarantee voting rights for black Americans, riots erupted in Watts, the black ghetto of Los Angeles, over a confrontation between a white policeman and a black driver. The riots, which would be replicated in other major cities later in the decade, expressed blacks' anger and frustration with their miserable living conditions, their limited access to jobs, and the police brutality that had become customary within black ghettos. In Watts, the rioting lasted for six days; cars and buildings were set on fire, and a battle between the rioters and the National Guard left thirty-four dead and more than one thousand injured. In July 1967 alone, 103 racial disorders erupted in the inner cities, five of which were full-scale riots.

Although Martin Luther King Jr. and other civil rights leaders condemned the riots because of their violence, many blacks were disillusioned by the idea that nonviolent resistance could bring about equality. The black power movement, galvanized by militant black nationalist Malcolm X, saw white America as its enemy. As a result, the black power movement adopted the attitude that black Americans must actively fight—using violence if necessary—to free themselves from the oppression of whites. As former civil rights activist Julius Lester writes,

> It slowly began to dawn on Negroes that whites didn't care quite as much about helping them get their freedom as they did about law and order. . . . The walls of segregation and discrimination were not crumbling and giving way to flowers of love and brotherhood. The walls were crumbling, but only to reveal a gigantic castle with walls ten times thicker than the walls of segregation. The castle was painted a brilliant white and lettered in bright red [was the word] Racism.[6]

## Conflict at Home and Abroad

Other groups besides blacks were also experiencing disillusionment with America—especially those activists who protested the Vietnam War. The war began in the late 1950s when President Dwight D. Eisenhower deployed a minimal number of troops to support South Vietnam against a communist takeover by North Vietnam. However, the desire to prevent the spread of communism—a desire that was created in part by the cold war hostility between the United States and the communist Soviet Union—influenced subsequent leaders to step up American intervention. Kennedy and Johnson both increased the number of troops in Vietnam, and by 1966, 267,000 U.S. troops were deployed there.

Dissenters, many of whom were students, disagreed with the war for a variety of reasons. Many felt that Vietnam was being used as a pawn in a larger struggle between the United States and its communist enemies. In addition, civilians and soldiers alike were appalled by the violent and unorthodox tactics—such as the use of flesh-burning napalm gas and the indiscriminate bombing of entire villages—employed by the American military in Vietnam. The war also became an issue for the civil rights movement when Martin Luther King Jr., in a speech delivered in 1967, brought attention to the fact that a preponderance of young black men were sent to the front lines of battle.

Television played a role in war opposition as well. For the first time in history, Americans were confronted with a vivid and often bloody portrait of the war. Images of battle, along with the numbers of casualties listed on television each night, made American families intimately aware of the war's human costs, which were rising with each year of conflict.

The first wave of antiwar protest began in the form of "teach-ins," group meetings during which the antiwar movement tried to educate people about why the war was wrong. However, as these methods failed to create change, antiwar protesters turned to more assertive means of protest, such as demonstrations and marches. As the war escalated, so did demonstrations against it. In 1965, fifteen thousand people in Berkeley marched against the war; at a New York rally in 1969, a million people expressed their dissent.

Adopting the civil rights movement's philosophy of civil disobedience, antiwar protesters by the thousands defied the military draft by publicly burning their draft cards. Civil disobedience against the war was often taken to dramatic levels, with protesters lying on railroad tracks to block trains carrying military troops and a few even committing suicide in front of government buildings. Some forms of protest went beyond civil disobedience, such as the ransacking of draft board files in order to prevent men from being drafted. These more controversial forms of protest provoked sharp criticism, especially from those Americans who questioned the propriety of antiwar protest in the first place.

## The Rise of Youth Counterculture

One of the most memorable examples of antiwar protest came in October 1967 when a group of thirty five thousand people, many of them hippies, surrounded the Pentagon building and attempted to "levitate" it as officials inside looked on with anger and disgust.

Although hippies were some of the most ardent peace activists of the decade, they also brought a spirit of humor and whimsy to the antiwar movement. In fact, the hippie movement had arisen in part to counteract the extreme seriousness of adult society. Hippies were, for the most part, college students and other youth who rebelled against the social conformity that had taken hold in the fifties. While they shared many beliefs with the New Left—especially views about the war—they did not believe, as SDS and other New Left groups did, that social or political change was a viable solution to the problems of America. For hippies, society *was* the problem. They saw the American lifestyle, with its emphasis on security, stability, and material prosperity, as inherently unfulfilling.

Hippies had been influenced in this view by the beat movement of the fifties, a group of artists and writers—including Jack Kerouac and Allen Ginsberg—who scorned marriage and traditional careers in favor of a more bohemian lifestyle. However, because a precedent for rebellion had been set by the civil rights movement and the antiwar protests, hippies drew a larger following than the beatniks. Hippie enclaves sprang up throughout the country, each with its own style of living. Some hippies, advocating a return to nature, established organic farms or vegetarian co-ops, while others became involved in urban cultural events such as poetry readings or experimental theater. Hippies dressed in unusual clothing—wearing everything from pirate costumes to peasant dresses to bellbottoms, flowers, and beads—took LSD and marijuana, promoted a philosophy of open sexuality or "free love," and filled parks and auditoriums to hear the music of Jefferson Airplane, the Grateful Dead, Quicksilver Messenger Service, the Byrds, and Janis Joplin.

## The Influence of Rock 'n' Roll

Rock music was a focal point of the era, not only for hippies but for youth in general. Although Elvis Presley was the first to introduce rock 'n' roll to the nation in the fifties, the musicians of the sixties established rock as a potent and indelible influence on American culture. Before the sixties, even rock music had conformed to societal standards, its lyrics confined to the innocent topic of young love. However, as social change and rebellion grew more prevalent in the midsixties, music began to reflect the widespread cultural dissent. In the early sixties, the Beatles sang "Love Me Do," but by the middle of the decade, they were expressing disillusionment with American society in "Revolution" and lauding LSD in "Lucy in the Sky with Diamonds." Music ultimately became a form of protest itself—especially the music of folksingers. Pete Seeger's "Where Have All the Flowers Gone?" made a powerful statement against the war, while Bob Dylan's "Blowin' in the Wind" spoke out on behalf of the civil rights movement.

Loud, rhythmic, and passionate, rock music provided a visceral outlet for emotional expression within the cautious and regulated world of adults. As one writer described it, rock 'n' roll "blows people all the way back to their senses and makes them feel good—like they're *alive* again in the middle of this monstrous funeral parlor of western civilization."[7]

In the eyes of many adults, however, rock music represented everything that was wrong with the values of the youth counterculture. Rock music seemed chaotic and brazenly sexual—even animalistic—to conservative Americans. Many criticized music festivals and other hippie events for providing what they saw as open forums for sexuality and drug use.

One of the most famous of these events was the "Summer of Love" in 1967. In January of that year, hippies had made a statement encouraging the youth of America to come to the Haight-Ashbury district of San Francisco "to affirm and celebrate a new spiritual dawn."[8] During that summer, the Haight became a hub of activity. Countercultural businesses and music venues flourished. The Monterey Pop Music Festival, the first major event of its kind, drew a crowd of over sixty thousand hippies.

However, the flood of young hippies arriving in Haight-Ashbury during the Summer of Love eventually became overwhelming. Many hippies could not find homes. Drug abuse was becoming more common within the Haight, as was rape and crime. The hippie movement itself began to become frustrated with what it had created, one member proclaiming that "Haight Street is just as bad as the squares say it is."[9] As a result, many hippies began to leave the city and form communes in the farmlands, some of which still exist today.

## Women's Liberation

While many young people found hippie communes to be an ideal form of living, the situation was not always so ideal for women. Just as in mainstream society, women in supposedly liberated hippie communities were often expected to do all of the cooking and cleaning. The civil rights movement and the New Left were also accused of relegating women to menial duties, while reserving ambitious projects for men. By the late sixties, a variety of female activists had announced that women needed to separate themselves from other movements and work for their own freedom.

Although the term did not appear until the late 1960s, the concept of women's liberation had appeared in the early sixties, when women began to challenge the idea that their place was in the home and not in the workplace. In 1963, Betty Friedan, in her famous book *The Feminine Mystique*, called for an end to the restrictive gender roles that were causing widespread discontent among suburban housewives. Friedan wanted to expand women's roles beyond those of wife and mother, as well as to change the laws and policies that limited women's career opportunities. To that end, Friedan and other feminists founded the National Organization for Women (NOW) in 1966.

However, to the young women of the hippie, civil rights, and antiwar movements, NOW's ideology and methods seemed too conservative. In the view of radical feminist organizations, which developed a few years after the formation of NOW, all American institutions, including marriage, were sexist. As Ellen Willis writes,

> Sexism, the [women's liberation] movement contended, was . . . embedded in law, tradition, economics, education, organized religion, science, language, the mass media, sexual morality, child rearing, the domestic division of labor, and everyday social interaction— whose intent and effect was to give men power over women. A sexist society enforced women's prescribed behavior with a wide range of sanctions that included social condemnation, ridicule, ostracism, sexual rejec-

tion and harassment, the withholding of birth control and abortion, economic deprivation, and male violence condoned by the state.[10]

Despite the differences between NOW and the more radical women's rights groups, the two factions often congregated at rallies. The sight of coiffed suburban housewives next to young women without makeup or bras was reminiscent of antiwar rallies, where clean-cut students dressed in shirts and ties marched alongside bearded hippies.

## The Tumult of 1968

The activism of the sixties came to a dramatic climax in 1968 with a series of stunning events. On April 4 of that year, Martin Luther King Jr. was assassinated in Memphis, Tennessee, a tragedy that set off a storm of race riots in 125 urban areas throughout the nation. A month later, President Johnson shocked the nation with an announcement that he

*Martin Luther King Jr. stands on the balcony of the Lorraine Motel, where he was assassinated a day later.*

would not seek reelection—an announcement that many saw as an admission that the Vietnam War had been a failure. Then, on June 5, 1968, only hours after winning the California Democratic primary for the presidency, Senator Robert F. Kennedy was assassinated. Later that summer, a nationally televised program showed Chicago police brutally attacking peace protesters outside the Democratic National Convention. Afraid that these events signaled a collapse of law and order, the nation responded with a renewed conservatism, and in November 1968, they elected a conservative Republican president, Richard Nixon.

However, despite the conservative trend of the nation, the youth of America celebrated hippie idealism at the Woodstock rock festival in 1969. Considered to be the last momentous sixties' event, Woodstock brought 400,000 people to the farmlands of New York for three days of rock music from artists such as Jimi Hendrix, the Grateful Dead, and the Who. The sheer enormity of the event created a variety of problems. Sanitation facilities broke down, food and water ran out, and a continuous traffic jam around the area meant that all musicians, food, and medical supplies had to be flown in by helicopter. However, according to participants, people responded to the crises with generosity and tolerance. As *Life* magazine wrote, "For nearly three days nearly half a million people lived elbow to elbow in the most exposed, crowded, rain-drenched, uncomfortable kind of community and there wasn't so much as a fist fight."[11] For others, the festival, with its drug use, nudity, and public sex, was nothing more than a garish example of the excesses of the hippie culture. Over the years, Woodstock has acquired an almost mythological status, representing for many Americans the essence of the sixties, both its positive and negative characteristics.

Woodstock was the last example of large-scale youth idealism. Within only a year, the country's mood would undergo a drastic change. Just as the decade began in protest, it ended with the 1970 demonstration at Kent State University, where a conflict between the National Guard and antiwar protesters left four students dead and nine wounded. The debacle at Kent State only fueled the antagonism between youth and adults and between antiwar protesters and the establishment. The antiwar protests of the 1960s continued until 1973, when President Richard Nixon finally called the last American troops home. Activism lived on in a variety of respects, most noticeably in the environmental, feminist, and gay liberation movements, but the unique spirit of rebellion that characterized the sixties activism lost momentum after the war's end.

## Raising Fundamental Questions

Although scholars, analysts, and sixties' children themselves disagree about the impact of the sixties, most people agree that the youth activism achieved what it set out to achieve. By challenging the conventions of the status quo, activists of the era forced Americans to reevaluate their values and their government. And, while political and social activism was not unique to the 1960s, never before in American history had the mood of revolt been so pervasive—nor had it ever involved such a diversity of issues. Historian David Chalmers argues that during the sixties,

> practically every classic social conflict or question erupted into the streets of the nation as a challenge to social stasis and stability; the individual vs. society; self-expression vs. authority, social justice vs. order, integration vs. separation, change vs. stability, reform vs. revolution, nonviolence vs. violence, spiritual values vs. materialism, and rationality vs. the irrational; war, peace, and the obligation to one's country; poverty, generational conflict, fathers and sons, black and white, empowerment, Chicanos, Native-Americans, male and female, lesbian and gay rights, sexual liberation, and the sensory exploration of the world of drugs.[12]

Whether or not these challenges to the status quo have benefited society is another question. Most people concede that the movements for racial and gender equality had positive goals and results. However, beyond this point of agreement, two conflicting views of the sixties have emerged. Some regard sixties activism as an affirmation of the democratic values of freedom and equality. According to writer William R. Garrett, the decade laid the groundwork "for addressing such impediments to full self-development as gender repression, racial discrimination, unfulfilling marriages, . . . and class barriers, which resulted in stultified lives."[13] Other analysts believe that the spirit of protest degenerated into purposeless rebellion and a quest for cheap thrills through sex and drugs. Morton A. Kaplan writes that "the generation of the sixties became a sea in which the extremists swam until their lack of self-control led to a collective . . . destructive dementia."[14] The very fact that the sixties still inspires such fervent controversy is proof that the impact of this tumultuous decade endures.

1. Quoted in Terry H. Anderson, *The Movement and the Sixties*. New York: Oxford University Press, 1995, p. 44.

2. Alexander Bloom and Wini Breines, eds., *"Takin' It to the Streets": A Sixties Reader*. New York: Oxford University Press, 1995, p. 5.

3. Quoted in Anderson, *The Movement and the Sixties*, p. 38.

4. Students for a Democratic Society, "Port Huron Statement," 1962, in William Dudley, ed., *The 1960s: Opposing Viewpoints*. San Diego: Greenhaven Press, 1997, p. 119.

5. Todd Gitlin, *The Sixties: Years of Hope, Days of Rage*. New York: Bantam Books, 1987, pp. 131–32.

6. Julius Lester, "The Angry Children of Malcolm X," in Dudley, *The 1960s: Opposing Viewpoints*, p. 178.

7. Quoted in Bloom and Breines, *"Takin' It to the Streets,"* p. 301.

8. Anderson, *The Movement and the Sixties*, p. 172.

9. Anderson, *The Movement and the Sixties*, p. 175.

10. Quoted in Alice Echols, *Daring to Be Bad: Radical Feminism in America, 1967–1975*. Minneapolis: University of Minnesota Press, 1989, p. ix.

11. Anderson, *The Movement and the Sixties*, p. 278.

12. Quoted in Dudley, *The 1960s: Opposing Viewpoints*, p. 17.

13. William R. Garrett, "Cultural Revolution and Character Formation," *World & I*, May 1998, p. 306.

14. Morton A. Kaplan, "The Misbegotten Sixties," *World & I*, May 1998, p. 317.

## CHAPTER 1

# Activism and Social Rebellion

*"Protests against the war are, in large part, responsible for prolonging it."*

# Americans Should Support the War in Vietnam

While the majority of the American public—69 percent as of 1969—support U.S. involvement in Vietnam, war dissenters have become increasingly visible as their tactics grow more radical. These "peaceful" tactics include vandalizing induction centers, burning draft cards, and physically threatening government officials or other supporters of the war. Protesters have created an atmosphere of discord in a country that needs, more than ever, unity and solidarity.

The intricacies of the Vietnam War can be difficult to understand, even for those who are embroiled in the conflict, but the war's central purpose is simple: The United States has intervened in Vietnam to prevent North Vietnam, led by the savage Viet Cong, from conquering South Vietnam and establishing a communist government.

The tactics that the Viet Cong has used to subjugate South Vietnam are barbaric. As South Vietnamese leader Ngo Dinh Diem attests,

> From the beginning, the Communists resorted to terror in their efforts to subvert our people, destroy our government, and impose a Communist regime

upon us. They have attacked defenseless teachers, closed schools, killed members of our anti-malarial program, and looted hospitals. This is coldly calculated to destroy our government's humanitarian efforts to serve our people.[1]

Furthermore, the Viet Cong directs most of its violence toward civilians. According to Lyndon B. Johnson, "Simple farmers are the targets of assassination and kidnapping. Women and children are strangled in the night because their men are loyal to their government. And helpless villages are ravaged by sneak attacks."[2]

## The Tyranny of Communism

The violence perpetrated by the communists in North Vietnam is typical of communism's philosophy of ruthlessness. Communism is a tyrannical form of government that abuses human rights and advocates violence. According to former president Dwight D. Eisenhower,

*President Lyndon B. Johnson greets troops of the Vietnam War. Johnson's unsuccessful war effort was the main reason he did not seek reelection in 1968.*

The communists' tactic of conquest by terror, their
callous disregard for human life, their philosophy
that the end justifies the means—no matter how bar-
barous and immoral the means may be—are precise-
ly the same in Vietnam as they have used in gobbling
up other countries and other free peoples of the
world. Their objectives have not changed or soft-
ened over the years. The only language they understand is force, or the threat of force.[3]

Communism is not only a danger to the people of Vietnam or
the nearby vicinity. Much like the Nazis, the communists' end
goal is to establish their regime worldwide by systematically
conquering free nations. The fact that North Vietnam
receives virtually all of its weapons and war materials from
communist countries—primarily China, the Soviet Union,
and East Germany—is clear proof that the communists are
united in their plan of international conquest.

## Abandoning South Vietnam
## Would Be Unethical

For the United States to abandon South Vietnam in its
defense against the Viet Cong would be unethical for three
important reasons. First, it would constitute breaking
America's repeated pledge to support and defend South
Vietnam from its enemies—a pledge that has been offered by
U.S. presidents since 1954. Second, America would be shirk-
ing its moral duty to help protect peaceful, defenseless regions
when they risk subjugation from a hostile power.

Finally, the United States must fight the communists of North
Vietnam because it has a responsibility—to its own citizens and to
the world—to stop the spread of communism. Just as America was
obligated to help eradicate Hitler's regime of fascism and genocide, it must do everything in its power to prevent the similarly
oppressive force of communism from expanding. Failure to do so
would mean immediate danger for the free countries of Asia and

eventual danger for the entire world. As Eisenhower attests, "It would be grossly immoral not to resist a tyranny whose openly avowed purpose is to subjugate the earth—and particularly the United States of America."[4]

## Protesters Prolong the War

Because the Vietnam War is so important to international peace, it is difficult to see why anyone would oppose U.S. involvement in Vietnam. War dissenters frequently dismiss the war's necessity based on an idealistic notion that war should be avoided at all costs. However, if dissenters were really interested in peace, they would stop their protests, because protesters against the war are, in large part, responsible for prolonging it. Antiwar demonstrations signal to the Viet Cong that the U.S. military does not have the support of its citizens. Believing that the U.S. government might suddenly accede to the demands of protestors and withdraw its troops, the Viet Cong is motivated to continue fighting. As Mark Arnold, a student at Oberlin College, contends, "The only thing [antiwar] demonstrations can accomplish is to prolong unduly the United States involvement in Vietnam because they provide the Viet Cong with one last desperate hope of victory."[5]

Furthermore, antiwar protests weaken the military's ability to fight effectively. At a time when the brave soldiers in Vietnam are in desperate need of their country's support, they are instead the recipients of scorn. Those who make the courageous choice to honor their draft cards are met at induction centers by the jeers of rabid demonstrators. Men who risk their lives on a daily basis to serve their country must enter into battle with the knowledge that their country does not support them in return. As a result, the soldiers serving in Vietnam feel depressed, abandoned, and discouraged. According to Colonel Robert D. Heinl Jr., "Unsupported in their travail . . . distrusted, disliked, and often reviled by the public, the uniformed services today are places of agony for the loyal, silent professionals who doggedly hang on and try to keep the ship afloat."[6]

The antiwar demonstrators' refusal to support the brave American soldiers in Vietnam is cruel and unpatriotic. By weakening U.S. morale and strengthening the resolve of the Viet Cong, protesters are prolonging the war and contributing to the loss of lives in South Vietnam. Their acts are nothing less than treason.

1. Lyndon B. Johnson, Ngo Dinh Diem, and John F. Kennedy, "Washington's Man in Saigon: American Commitment to South Vietnam," *Department of State Bulletins*, June 19, 1961, in Marvin E. Gettleman, Jane Franklin, Marilyn Young, and H. Bruce Franklin, eds., *Vietnam and America: A Documented History*. New York: Grove Press, 1985, p. 163.

2. Lyndon B. Johnson's speech at Johns Hopkins University, April 7, 1965, in William Dudley, ed., *The 1960s: Opposing Viewpoints*. San Diego: Greenhaven Press, 1997, p. 85.

3. Dwight D. Eisenhower, "Let's Close Ranks on the Home Front," *Reader's Digest*, April 1968, in Dudley, *The 1960s: Opposing Viewpoints*, p. 112.

4. Eisenhower, "Let's Close Ranks on the Home Front," in Dudley, *The 1960s: Opposing Viewpoints*, p. 109.

5. Quoted in Dudley, *The 1960s: Opposing Viewpoints*, p. 110.

6. Colonel Robert D. Heinl Jr., "The Collapse of the Armed Forces," *Armed Forces Journal*, June 7, 1971, in Gettleman et al., *Vietnam and America*, p. 323.

*"Protest is the country's only hope of restoring American values and putting a stop to the menace in Vietnam."*

# Americans Should Oppose the War in Vietnam

U.S. officials contend that the purpose of the Vietnam War is to protect South Vietnam from North Vietnam's "communist tyranny." This claim gravely misrepresents the truth. The war in Vietnam began as an indigenous political revolt supported by Vietnamese people in the North *and* the South. This revolt was a reaction against South Vietnamese dictator Ngo Dinh Diem, who, in 1956, abolished free elections and set up concentration camps for all political opponents. Although the United States labels this revolt as "communist"—its catchword for "dangerous"—a mere 25 percent of the Vietnamese rebels consider themselves to be communist.

The United States intervened in this conflict on behalf of South Vietnam only because America's communist enemies, the Soviet Union and China, had declared their support for North Vietnam. Both sides—the United States and the communist powers—are using Vietnam as a pawn in a power struggle between democracy and communism. The United States is trying to squelch the revolution in Vietnam in order to prove its military superiority to that of the communist countries. It has no authentic concern for the welfare of Vietnam.

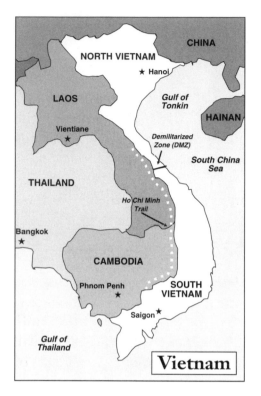

**Vietnam**

In fact, in recent history, the United States took a vigorous role in suppressing Vietnam's freedom. During the years between 1945 and 1954, the American government helped finance France's unsuccessful attempt to recolonize Vietnam. Although Vietnam quoted the American Declaration of Independence when it proclaimed independence from France in 1945, the U.S. government callously disregarded Vietnam's desire for freedom.

Now, under the guise of supporting freedom in Vietnam, the United States is carrying out a selfish and immoral political agenda. It supports corrupt South Vietnamese dictators, such as Diem, who eradicate political opposition with violence. It condones the daily murder of Vietnamese civilians, many of them killed by the U.S. Army's flesh-burning napalm gas. It has become South Vietnam's oppressor, not its protector. As Martin Luther King Jr. says,

> [The South Vietnamese] languish under our bombs and consider us—not their fellow Vietnamese—the real enemy. They move sadly and apathetically as we herd them off the land of their fathers into concentration camps where minimal social needs are rarely met. They know they must move or be destroyed by our bombs. . . . They watch as we poison their water, as we kill a million acres of their crops. They must weep as the bulldozers destroy their precious trees.

They wander into the hospitals, with at least 20 casualties from American firepower for each Viet Cong–inflicted injury. So far we may have killed a million of them—mostly children.[1]

Despite these atrocities, U.S. officials still insist that the war in Vietnam is noble and necessary. They refuse to consider retreating because to do so would be to admit defeat. Sadly, America's military pride takes precedence over the hundreds of young American men and Vietnamese civilians who are killed each day in Vietnam.

## The Need for a Massive Social Movement

Because U.S. officials are determined to continue the war despite its destructive consequences, it is up to American citizens to end the war by protest. A social uprising is the only way to send a message to the government that its actions will not be tolerated. According to Paul Potter, president of Students for a Democratic Society,

> If the people of this country are to end the war in Vietnam, and to change the institutions which create it, then the people of this country must create a massive social movement. . . . The reason the war and the system it represents will be stopped, if it is stopped before it destroys all of us, will be because the movement has become strong enough to exact change in the society. Twenty thousand people, . . . if they were serious, if they were willing to . . . commit themselves to building a movement wherever they are and in whatever way they effectively can, would be . . . enough.[2]

If the government cannot be motivated to change its course by intellectual arguments, emotional pleas, or collective action, then its citizens must make it literally impossible for the war to continue. Refusing the draft is the most direct means by which the American people can bring about an end to the war, since without soldiers, the war cannot be fought. Evading the draft through deferments—legal waivers of military service that are frequently offered to college students—is one way that young men have expressed their feelings about the war; however, legal means are not enough. The Resistance, a group of men who have pledged to refuse the draft by illegal means, explain why protestors must actively challenge the war through civil disobedience:

> We of the Resistance feel that we can no longer passively acquiesce to the Selective Service System by accepting its deferments. . . . Legal draft alternatives are kept within reach of elite groups—good students, those who are able to express objection to all war on religious grounds, and those with the money to hire good lawyers. For the majority of American guys the only alternatives are jail or the army. While those who are most opposed to the war have been silenced, the system that provides the personnel for war crimes continues to function smoothly.[3]

The most significant of the many illegal antidraft activities has been the 1967 siege on the Pentagon, during which fifty-thousand people rallied in Washington and incited a spontaneous mass burning of draft cards. Combat troops in Vietnam have lent support to these activities by organizing collective efforts to desert the war. These acts of civil disobedience demonstrate to the government that its citizens will not be a part of its military schemes, no matter what the consequences. If enough people are willing to participate in these acts, the government will have to capitulate: It can only imprison so many protesters.

## Antiwar Protest Expresses Faith in America

Some claim that antiwar protest is unpatriotic and view the draft-card burnings and desertions as a desecration of our nation's honor. But in truth, those who protest the war are expressing their faith in America, not as a great military power but as an example of democracy and freedom. As Senator J. William Fulbright observes, "All [war dissenters] believe that their country was cut out for something more ennobling than imperial destiny. Our youth are showing that they still believe in the American dream, and their protests attest to its continuing vitality."[4] Protest is the country's only hope of restoring American values and putting a stop to the menace in Vietnam.

1. Martin Luther King Jr., "Declaration of Independence from the War in Vietnam," 1967, in Marvin E. Gettleman, Jane Franklin, Marilyn Young, and H. Bruce Franklin, eds., *Vietnam and America: A Documented History*. New York: Grove Press, 1985, pp. 310–11.

2. Paul Potter, "The Incredible War," April 17, 1965, in Alexander Bloom and Wini Breines, eds., *"Takin' It to the Streets": A Sixties Reader*. New York: Oxford University Press, 1995, p. 218.

3. The Resistance, "We Refuse—October 16," in Michael Ferber and Staughton Lynd, *The Resistance*. Boston: Beacon Press, 1971, p. 90.

4. J. William Fulbright, "The Great Society Is a Sick Society," *New York Times Magazine*, August 20, 1967, in William Dudley, ed., *The 1960s: Opposing Viewpoints*. San Diego: Greenhaven Press, 1997, p. 101.

*"[Hippies] are congregating—in big cities, small towns, and the countryside—in order to explore a simpler, more fulfilling way of living."*

# Hippies Are Creating a Desirable Social Revolution

American adults commonly disparage hippies as a group of "freaks." However, if anything, this term is more fitting for the members of mainstream society. The lifestyle of middle-class Americans is both absurd and dehumanizing. Most of them wake up every morning at an appointed time, put on their identical business suits, and confine themselves to an artificial environment for eight hours a day. More often than not, their job gives them no intellectual or emotional satisfaction, yet they spend over a third of their lives at the workplace. They endure this dismal existence for one reason: money. Ironically, the more wealth and possessions they acquire, the more dissatisfied they are with what they have. As writer Guy Strait says,

> The terrible truth about our prosperity is that it is the bringer of misery. We have been brainwashed by the advertising industry into being the most dissatisfied people in the world. We are told we must all be handsome or beautiful, sexually devastating, and the owners of a staggering amount of recreational gadgetry or doomed to frustration. The result is that

most of us are frustrated. It is exactly this that the hippie avoids like poison. He wants no part of self-defeating goals.[1]

Hippies are repulsed by this greedy, materialistic society. Determined not to repeat the mistakes of their parents, hippies have dropped out of mainstream culture. They are congregating—in big cities, small towns, and the countryside—in order to explore a simpler, more fulfilling way of living.

## What Are Hippies?

Sonny, a hippie living in the East Village in New York, says that

The hippies [are] people who've dropped [societal] hangups. People who can behave as children when they want to, unashamedly. . . . Swing from light posts, climb trees. People who aren't afraid of loving each other. People who aren't suspicious.[2]

Unlike most other groups, hippie culture has no particular rules, agenda, or lifestyle. Some hippies live and work together in communal households—doing things such as farming, canning fruits, or building furniture. Others are nomads who stay briefly at one locale and then move on. Still others are political activists, artists, or students.

## Freedom from Money

Whatever their lifestyle, all hippies reject materialism. In hippie communities, money is never an issue because sharing allows everyone to meet their basic needs of food and shelter. The freedom from materialistic goals unburdens people from the repressive, mind-numbing workday, allowing them to do what makes them happiest. In Sonny's words,

It's plausible to envision a society where everybody could just go out and "do their own thing." The only way that could work . . . is if you do away with the whole concept of pay. These ideas are working now [on hippie communes]. . . . If you dig farming, you give the food away, except for what you need to eat. If you're making things—chairs, tables, or anything like that—you give them away to those who need it. And if you need help on something, you just ask somebody, "Hey, I'm doing this today," and so they come and help you. It's. . . a total sharing.[3]

Not only does sharing eliminate the need for the traditional workday, but it also helps to create friendships based on mutual cooperation and generosity. When people are not competing with each other for jobs, money, or spouses, they are able to love each other without reservations. This is what is meant by "free love." Free love has no restrictions or contingencies, nor is it limited to one person or one gender. Sex is an expression of this love, and it should be shared and celebrated, not parceled out stingily in return for a monogamous

*In 1967, hippies smoked marijuana openly in the Haight-Ashbury district of San Francisco.*

commitment or marriage. As Ron Norman says, "Make love—not to one [person] who you grab onto and possess out of fear and loneliness—but to all beautiful people, all sexes, all ages."[4]

Free love also fosters a spirit of community—a spirit that has been all but obliterated from most people's lives. The majority of American families reside in suburban homes, which keep them so isolated that neighbors of ten years often barely know each other. Communal living, on the other hand, promotes interaction and love among people. One of the best examples of communal living on a large scale is the Woodstock music festival of 1969. In August 1969, 400,000 hippies gathered in the farmlands of upstate New York to celebrate three days of peace, love, and rock 'n' roll. When rain turned the area into a swamp of red mud, supplies ran low, and sanitation facilities broke down, newscasters described the event as a catastrophe. However, those who attended the festival called it beautiful. In a situation that would ordinarily breed riots, there was cooperation, not violence. People pooled their resources, shared food and other amenities, cared for the sick, danced to the music, and enjoyed being alive. For the three days that it existed, Woodstock was an ideal community, a group of people from all over the country, of different ages and backgrounds, living together in harmony—despite stressful circumstances. As one hippie explains, "Woodstock is the great example of how it is going to be in the future. . . . The loving and the peaceful are the majority. . . .We are winning."[5]

## Destroying the Jungle of Taboos

Unfortunately, not everyone was able to understand what Woodstock had achieved. Media pundits and other squares railed against the festival, calling it a show of "mass infantilism." They found Woodstock appalling, in part because it defied the societal "rule" that love should be confined to the family. This rule, however, is merely a social taboo—one of the many that permeate American culture. Mainstream society is, as Strait says, "a jungle of taboos."[6] These taboos regulate every aspect of life, dictating people's physical appearance and behavior, and are so deeply ingrained within American consciousness that any behavior diverging from them is immediately considered "wrong."

One of the strictest and most unacknowledged taboos in American society relates to dress. Social conventions demand that businessmen have short hair and a clean-shaven face and wear a suit and tie; women are required to wear makeup, skirts, and high-heeled shoes. These uniforms signal to the rest of society a desire to "fit in." Anyone whose appearance fails to conform to these ideals is immediately distrusted or ridiculed. In fact, the angriest criticism of hippies centers on their long hair and unique clothing.

People in society are conditioned by social taboos to the extent that they are completely unable to make decisions for themselves. Take drug use, for instance. There's no logical reason why alcohol, a mind-altering drug that commonly inspires aggression in its users, is socially acceptable, while marijuana, a mind-altering drug that produces feelings of euphoria and relaxation, is not. Distinctions such as these are arbitrary social norms, nothing more.

Within hippie culture, LSD, a hallucinogenic drug, is commonly used for the spiritual purpose of bringing people closer to each other and to a higher being. LSD has the ability to encourage introspection, serenity, and, as one writer says, "an unusual unification of the mind, soul, and the senses."[7] However, this approach to religion is instantly dismissed by most Americans as invalid. Somehow, the traditional ritual of "getting up on Sunday morning, going down to a mortgaged building, and staring at the back of somebody's neck"[8] is deemed more worthy than utilizing the significant power of LSD. For most Americans, religion is—like school, work, and family—a duty, not a celebration.

## Reclaiming the Freedom of Choice

It is sad that as society's boundaries of knowledge and technology are constantly traversing new limits, its members are still enslaved by archaic notions of how people should live and act. Laws or social conventions that limit people's freedom are wrong and go against the American ideals of democracy and individualism. Hippies break these conventions in order to reclaim the freedom of choice that all people are entitled to, and to celebrate the innumerable ways in which people can find happiness.

1. Guy Strait, "What Is a Hippie?" 1967, in Alexander Bloom and Wini Breines, eds., *"Takin' It to the Streets": A Sixties Reader.* New York: Oxford University Press, 1995, p. 312.

2. Sonny, interviewed by Lewis Yablonsky, *The Hippie Trip*, 1968, in William Dudley, ed., *The 1960s: Opposing Viewpoints.* San Diego: Greenhaven Press, 1997, p. 138.

3. Sonny, interviewed by Yablonsky, *The Hippie Trip*, 1968, in Dudley, ed. *The 1960s: Opposing Viewpoints*, p. 139.

4. Quoted in Timothy Miller, *The Hippies and American Values.* Knoxville: University of Tennessee Press, 1991, p. 50.

5. Quoted in Terry H. Anderson, *The Movement and the Sixties.* New York: Oxford University Press, 1995, pp. 278–79.

6. Strait, "What Is a Hippie?" in Bloom and Breines, *"Takin' It to the Streets,"* p. 310.

7. *Washington Free Press*, quoted in Miller, *The Hippies and American Values*, p. 37.

8. Timothy Miller, quoted in Dudley, *The 1960s: Opposing Viewpoints*, p. 140.

*"The real goal of hippie culture seems to be a sexual free-for-all, where people's bodies are merely objects to be used and discarded."*

# Hippies Are a Harmful Influence on America's Youth

Across the nation, groups of young people have become known as hippies. What exactly are hippies? Most ordinary adults won't encounter many, because hippies can't be found working to support a family or defending their country in the armed services. Hippies rarely do anything at all except laze around parks or city streets taking drugs. In a different era, one would have simply called them bums.

Certainly they bear a physical resemblance to bums. Commenting on the unmistakable hippie appearance, California governor Ronald Reagan said that a hippie is some-one who "dresses like Tarzan, has hair like Jane, and smells like Cheetah."[1] If it weren't for the shaggy, foot-long beards on most hippie men, it would be impossible to distinguish the males from the females. The men wear their hair down to their waists, while the women run around with unshaven legs, uncombed hair, and no cosmetics or brassieres.

## A Danger to American Youth

The freakish appearance of hippies alarms most adults, and it should, because the culture poses a serious danger to

America's youth. Influenced by the hippie rhetoric that calls mainstream society "evil," thousands of impressionable youth have abandoned their schools, jobs, and homes. Some as young as fourteen have deserted their families in order to take up with the hippies.

Like any cult, the youth counterculture makes false promises in order to gain adherents. It claims to offer a life free of the financial and social pressures of the modern world. Furthermore, it plays to teenagers' craving for acceptance from their peers by portraying itself as a loving, harmonious community.

What the hippie movement actually delivers is another matter altogether. Unfortunately, hippies learn the hard way that work and responsibility are an essential part of survival. Young hippies, drawn to the culture by its promise of an easy life, often end up living on the streets, scavenging for even the most basic sustenance. Some suffer prolonged, agonizing deaths of starvation. Others are done in by fatal drug overdoses.

## Promoting Drugs

Overdoses are common because, in hippie communities, drugs are usually more accessible than food. Hippies promote drugs as the solution to any and every problem—including problems caused by drug use in the first place. Acid, a potent hallucinogenic drug also known as LSD, is the hippie drug of choice. As one writer says,

> [Hippies] believe that acid is the answer & neither know nor care what the question is. They think dope is the easy road to God.
>
> "Have you ever been raped?" they say. "Take acid & everything'll be groovy.
>
> "Are you ill? Take acid & find inner health.
>
> "Are you cold, sleeping in doorways at night? Take acid & discover your own inner warmth.

"Are you hungry? Take acid and transcend those mundane needs."[2]

What hippies refuse to acknowledge is that acid is an extremely dangerous drug. Used over an extended period of time, it is so powerful that it can induce psychosis. In the short term it can be just as harmful. While on LSD, some people experience terrifying hallucinations, such as the belief that they are completely covered with tarantulas or that someone is trying to kill them. These hallucinations can be so traumatic that users will try to commit suicide as a way to escape them.

The leaders of the hippie movement casually dismiss these incidents as "bad trips." They continue to pump young hippies full of LSD, all the while feeding them lies about the drug's beneficial properties. Timothy Leary, a former Harvard professor who dosed his own students with LSD for

*Former Harvard professor Timothy Leary advocated the use of LSD for its mind-altering properties.*

"research" purposes, even has the nerve to claim that drugs are the route to spiritual fulfillment. In touting this notion, Leary conveniently provides young people with rationalization for behavior that is both dangerous and wrong.

The motive behind the actions of Leary and other counterculture promoters is—big surprise—money. Leary himself receives $3.50 a head for lectures that he gives advocating LSD. In addition, he holds two-week LSD "seminars" for paying customers. Who knows how much more he gets from the sale of drugs themselves?

## A Culture of Promiscuity

Another dangerous feature of the hippie culture is sexual promiscuity, which usually goes under the euphemism of "free love." The real goal of hippie culture seems to be a sexual free-for-all, where people's bodies are merely objects to be used and discarded.

The hippies' rock music festivals are clear evidence of this. One writer described a Beatles rock concert he observed as "an orgy for teenagers."[3] A radio personality, writing about a 1964 music festival, said that "the entire evening seemed *designed* to arouse every animal and sex instinct in the audience up to an uncontrollable pitch and just such did it accomplish."[4]

The hippie culture of promiscuity is seriously damaging— particularly for girls and young women. Told by lustful hippie men that sexual abstinence is "repressive," women feel obligated to engage in sex that they don't want. Robin Morgan says that "at [hippie music festivals] Woodstock or Alamont a woman could be declared uptight or a poor sport if she didn't want to be raped."[5]

The manipulation of women isn't always psychological. Some women have been plied with drugs and then gang-raped by a group of hippie men. One writer describes the fate of a young girl drawn to Haight Street, a dirty, impoverished section of San Francisco where hippies congregate:

Pretty little 16-year-old middle-class chick comes to the Haight to see what it's all about and gets picked up by a 17-year-old street dealer who spends all day shooting her full of speed again and again, then feeds her 3,000 mikes [micrograms of speed, twelve times the regular dose] and raffles her temporarily unemployed body for the biggest Haight Street gang bang since night before last. . . Rape is as common as bullshit on Haight Street.[6]

The combination of drug use and promiscuity can only lead to more horrific scenarios such as this one. It is time for hippie society to be exposed for what it is, a perverse culture of self-gratification, before more young people are drawn into its destructive lifestyle.

1. Quoted in Todd Gitlin, *The Sixties: Years of Hope, Days of Rage*. New York: Bantam Books, 1987, p. 217.

2. Communications Company, "Uncle Tim'$ Children," undated handbill distributed in the late sixties in the Haight-Ashbury district of San Francisco, in William Dudley, ed., *The 1960s: Opposing Viewpoints*. San Diego: Greenhaven Press, 1997, p. 150.

3. Bernard Saibel, quoted in Rev. David A. Noebel, "Rhythm, Riots, and Revolution," in Alexander Bloom and Wini Breines, *"Takin' It to the Streets": A Sixties Reader*. New York: Oxford University Press, 1995, p. 379.

4. Burt McMurtrie, quoted in Noebel, "Rhythm, Riots and Revolution," in Bloom and Breines, *"Takin' It to the Streets,"* p. 378.

5. Robin Morgan, "Goodbye to All That," in Bloom and Breines, *"Takin' It to the Streets,"* p. 501.

6. Communications Company, "Uncle Tim'$ Children," in Dudley, *The 1960s: Opposing Viewpoints*, p. 149.

## CHAPTER 2

# Movements for Equality

*"In imagining and articulating a free society for blacks, the civil rights movement takes the first step toward achieving it."*

# The Civil Rights Movement Helps Blacks Achieve Equality

In 1896, in *Plessy v. Ferguson*, the Supreme Court upheld a Louisiana law requiring blacks and whites to sit in separate railway cars, maintaining that racial segregation was merely a system of "separate but equal" facilities. However, Justice John Marshall Harlan, the sole dissenting voice in *Plessy v. Ferguson*, recognized that segregation was inherently unequal: "What can more certainly arouse race hate, . . . than state enactments, which . . . proceed on the ground that colored citizens are so inferior and degraded that they cannot be allowed to sit [with] white citizens? That . . . is the real meaning of such legislation."[1]

Sadly, more than fifty years after Harlan wrote these words, segregation still thrives in American society. In the South, Jim Crow laws mandate separate facilities—including schools, hospitals, restaurants, drinking fountains, and even morgues—for blacks and whites. A little black girl living in Mississippi cannot visit the whites-only circus that has come to her town.

Nor can she attend the local high school that might best prepare her for college. Anywhere her family travels in the South, they are required to enter restaurants through the back door—if they are allowed inside at all—and they must sleep in their car because no motel will accept them.

Clearly, if America is to live up to its promise of equality for all people, this unjust system of ostracism must be ended. As Martin Luther King Jr. says, "Now is the time to make real the promises of Democracy. Now is the time to rise from the dark and desolate valley of segregation to the sunlit path of racial justice. Now is the time to open the doors of opportunity to all of God's children. Now is the time to lift our nation from the quicksands of racial injustice to the solid rock of brotherhood."[2]

## Origins of the Movement

The civil rights movement has arisen out of a commitment on the part of an increasing number of people—both blacks and whites—to take direct, immediate action against segregation, discrimination, and other forms of racial prejudice. The movement unofficially began in 1955, when Rosa Parks, a black lady riding a bus in Montgomery, Alabama, refused to move to the back of the bus to make room for a white man who had boarded. Her subsequent arrest incited a storm of fury within the black community of Montgomery. Its leaders, among them a young minister named Martin Luther King Jr., organized a boycott of the Montgomery bus system to protest the incident. For an entire year, from December 1955 to December 1956, blacks walked, bicycled, or carpooled to work. The impact of the boycott was tremendous. Not only did it exact a serious financial toll on Montgomery's racist bus system, but it also inspired other types of civil rights activism throughout the country.

Led by King, people in cities all over the nation began to resist or protest unjust laws and practices. In 1960, four black students in Greensboro, North Carolina, sat down at a whites-only Woolworth's lunch counter and refused to leave until served, inventing a form of protest now known as a sit-in. The following year, a group of black and white men calling themselves the Freedom Riders rode an interstate bus from Washington, D.C., to New Orleans—braving violent, racist mobs along the way—to desegregate bus stations throughout the South.

## Nonviolent Direct Action

These protests are examples of nonviolent direct action, a collective, organized form of activism that includes boycotts, picketing, demonstrations, and sit-ins. The predominant method of action within the civil rights movement, nonviolent direct action is a powerful impetus for change. These protests force both blacks and whites to think about the unequal status of blacks in America. For example, when a group of civil rights supporters enters a whites-only restaurant and asks to be served, the restaurant owners, patrons, and the local public cannot easily ignore or dismiss them. Instead, they must find a way of dealing with the activists' demands. As Martin Luther

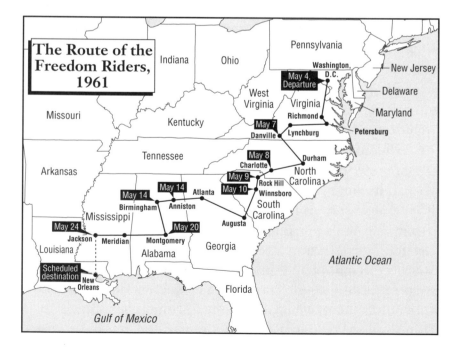

King Jr. states, "Nonviolent direct action seeks to create such a crisis and foster such a tension that a community which has constantly refused to negotiate is forced to confront the issue. It seeks so to dramatize the issue that it can no longer be ignored."[3] The more people involved in the action, the better chance that it will be noticed and dealt with.

## The Importance of Nonviolence

However, as sit-ins and demonstrations have grown in number and scope, racist police and citizens have attempted to quell the protests with force. When attacked, civil rights workers will adopt a fetal position, blocking their faces with their hands. In this position many have been severely beaten—a few have even been killed—with crowbars or clubs. In light of these ruthless displays of violence, retaliation is tempting. However, violence is not feasible from a practical standpoint, nor is it acceptable from a moral one. A violent approach to gaining equality will only lead to more violence, resulting in a bloody battle from which both sides will emerge full of rage and antipathy. Nonviolence, on the other hand, has the power to transform people's attitudes. As the Student Nonviolent Coordinating Committee says,

> Through nonviolence, courage displaces fear; love transforms hate. Acceptance dissipates prejudice; hope ends despair. Peace dominates war; faith reconciles doubt. Mutual regard cancels enmity. Justice for all overthrows injustice.[4]

## A Christian Ethic

Guided by this Christian ethic of love and hope, civil rights activists are striving to create a better society for all Americans. This Christian spirit has come to be the most important—and most inspiring—characteristic of the civil rights movement. With its message of optimism and faith, it allows people to envision a better world, a world in which blacks and whites live together in harmony and equality. In imagining and articulating a free society for blacks, the civil rights movement takes the first step toward achieving it. Martin Luther King Jr. in "I Have a Dream," his famous 1963 speech, describes what such a world would be like:

> I have a dream that one day this nation will rise up and live out the true meaning of its creed: "We hold these truths to be self-evident: that all men are created equal." . . . I have a dream that one day on the red hills of Georgia the sons of former slaves and the sons of former slaveowners will be able to sit down together at a table of brotherhood. I have a dream that one day even the state of Mississippi, a desert state, sweltering with the heat of injustice and oppression, will be transformed into an oasis of freedom and justice.[5]

1. Justice John Harlan, dissenting opinion in *Plessy v. Ferguson*, 1896. www.geocities.com/CapitolHill/8569/plessy.v.ferguson.html.

2. Martin Luther King Jr., "I Have a Dream," August 28, 1963, in Peter B. Levy, ed., *Let Freedom Ring: A Documentary History of the Modern Civil Rights Movement*. New York: Praeger, 1992, p. 123.

3. Martin Luther King Jr., "Letter from Birmingham Jail," April 16, 1963, in Sylvan Barnet and Hugo Bedau, eds., *Critical Thinking, Reading, and Writing: A Brief Guide to Argument*. 3rd ed. New York: St. Martin's Press, 1999, p. 433.

4. Student Nonviolent Coordinating Committee, "Statement of Purpose," April 1960, in Levy, *Let Freedom Ring*, p. 74.

5. Martin Luther King Jr., "I Have a Dream," August 28, 1963. http://web66.coled.umn.edu/new/MLK/MLK.html.

*"[The assassination of Martin Luther King Jr.] is clear
proof that nonviolence will never bring equality for blacks."*

# The Civil Rights Movement Does Not Help Blacks Achieve Equality

On April 4, 1968, as Martin Luther King Jr., leader of the civil rights movement, stood on the balcony of the Lorraine Motel in Memphis, he was shot through the head and killed by a white assassin.

The assassination of Martin Luther King Jr. is, and should be, the end of the civil rights movement in America. King's death is clear proof that nonviolence will never bring equality for blacks. As Black Panther leader Eldridge Cleaver states,

> The assassin's bullet not only killed Dr. King, it killed a period of history. It killed a hope, and it killed a dream. That white America could produce the assassin of Dr. Martin Luther King is looked upon by black people—and not just those identified as black militants—as a final repudiation by white America of any hope of reconciliation, of any hope of change by peaceful and nonviolent means.[1]

For many in the black community, King's death was no surprise. White society has shown again and again that it is determined to keep blacks in an inferior position—and that it will use any and all types of violence to do so. Those who have peacefully protested segregation have had their skulls beaten with billy clubs and crowbars, their faces kicked, and tear gas sprayed into their eyes. Outspoken black leaders have been shot while sleeping next to their wives at night or have awoken to find their homes on fire. At civil rights demonstrations, racist white mobs chant, "I wish I was an Alabama deputy, so I could kill a nigger legally."[2]

Even innocent black children are the targets of white violence. In Money, Mississippi, fourteen-year-old Emmett Till, who allegedly whistled at a white woman, was dragged out of his home, beaten until mutilated, and then shot in the head at point-blank range. On September 15, 1963, four young black girls, dressed in their Sunday white, were killed when a bomb exploded at the Sixteenth Street Baptist Church in Birmingham, Alabama.

## By Any Means Necessary

The belief that peaceful civil rights demonstrations can persuade whites to end these hideous acts of violence is naïve. Malcolm X, the most powerful and articulate black speaker in America until his assassination in 1965, explains,

> If we could bring about recognition and respect for our people by peaceful means, well and good. Everybody would like to reach his objectives peacefully. But I'm also a realist. The only people in this country who are asked to be nonviolent are black people. I've never heard anybody go to the Ku Klux Klan and teach them nonviolence. . . . I don't go along with anyone who wants to teach our people nonviolence until someone at the same time is teaching our enemy to be nonviolent.[3]

Blacks, in the words of Malcolm X, must defend themselves against acts of racial violence "by any means necessary"[4]—even if those means include force.

## Demanding Freedom

Furthermore, blacks must not ask for their rights but *demand* them. Blacks do not need whites to grant them rights; they have rights whether or not any white person says they do. As Malcolm X puts it, "There's no white man going to tell me anything about my rights. . . . If it doesn't take senators and congressmen and presidential proclamations to give freedom to the white man, it is not necessary for legislation or proclamation or Supreme Court decisions to give freedom to the black man."[5]

The rights that blacks must claim include full employment, access to decent housing and education, an immediate end to police brutality, and a guarantee that blacks will be tried in

*Leaders of the Black Panther organization stand guard outside their headquarters. Such militant groups arose when blacks became disillusioned with nonviolent equality movements.*

court by a jury of their peers. Furthermore, blacks should not be required to serve in the military to defend a government that refuses to protect them from racist violence, nor should they be held prisoners by a criminal justice system that does not give them fair trials.

Finally, blacks must demand financial compensation for the years that they were forced to work as slaves. The Black Panther Party explains why blacks have an undeniable right to restitution:

> We believe that this racist government has robbed us and now we are demanding the overdue debt of forty acres and two mules. Forty acres and two mules was promised 100 years ago as restitution for slave labor and mass murder of black people. We will accept the payment as currency which will be distributed to our many communities. . . . The American racist has taken part in the slaughter of over twenty million black people; therefore, we feel that this is a modest demand that we make.[6]

## The Role of Riots

Blacks must take an active stance toward securing these demands. Rioting is the most forceful and effective way that blacks can repudiate racist violence and oppression. By creating fear and disorder within urban communities, riots interrupt the status quo to the point where change must occur. According to Tom Hayden,

> Persistent, accurately-aimed attacks, which need not be on human life to be effective, might disrupt the administration of the ghetto to a crisis point where a new system would have to be considered.[7]

Most whites, both liberals and conservatives alike, assume that rioting is wrong because it is lawless behavior. However, this assumption ignores the fact that for centuries blacks have lived in a society where laws have been the tools of institutionalized slavery and racism. As Hayden explains, "To the people involved, the riot is far less lawless and far more representative than the system of arbitrary rules and prescribed channels which they confront every day."[8]

Others protest that violent revolt will never bring reconciliation between blacks and whites. However, racial healing is irrelevant to blacks at this point in history, and it will remain irrelevant until their basic rights are recognized. And, as Cleaver contends, it is more than obvious that "the only way for black people in this country to get the things that they want—and the things that they have a right to and that they deserve—is to meet fire with fire."[9]

1. Eldridge Cleaver, "Requiem for Nonviolence," *Ramparts Magazine*, 1968, in Alexander Bloom and Wini Breines, eds., *"Takin' It to the Streets": A Sixties Reader.* New York: Oxford University Press, 1995, p. 171.

2. Quoted in Julius Lester, "The Angry Children of Malcolm X," in William Dudley, ed., *The 1960s: Opposing Viewpoints.* San Diego: Greenhaven Press, 1997, p. 179.

3. Malcolm X, *By Any Means Necessary.* New York: Pathfinder, 1992, p. 160.

4. Malcolm X, *By Any Means Necessary*, p. 34.

5. Malcolm X, "The Ballot or Bullet," 1965, in Bloom and Breines, *"Takin' It to the Streets,"* p. 141.

6. The Black Panther Platform, 1966. http://lists.village.virginia.edu/sixties/HTML_docs/ Resources/Primary/Manifestos/Panther_platform.html.

7. Tom Hayden, *Rebellion in Newark*, 1967, in Dudley, *The 1960s: Opposing Viewpoints*, p. 194.

8. Hayden, *Rebellion in Newark*, in Dudley, *The 1960s: Opposing Viewpoints*, p. 193.

9. Cleaver, "Requiem for Nonviolence," in Bloom and Breines, *"Takin' It to the Streets,"* p. 171.

*"Because the women's liberation movement aims to reform [social] roles for both sexes, it will improve society for men as well as women."*

# The Women's Liberation Movement Benefits Women and Men

Less than one hundred years ago, women in America were regarded as second-class citizens. They could not vote, attend college, or work in most professions; in some places, they were even required to turn over their property and possessions to their husbands or male relatives. Women's rights groups of the early 1900s worked hard to counter these injustices through legislative reform. Although their work eliminated most legal inequities, women's status in society is still unequal to that of men. In the 1960s, the actual situation of women is poor—and some evidence suggests that it is growing worse. The National Organization for Women, writing in 1966, reports that

> Although 46.4 percent of all American women between the ages of eighteen and sixty-five now work outside the homes, the overwhelming majority—75 percent—are in routine clerical, sales, or factory jobs, or they are household workers, cleaning women, hospital attendants. . . . Working women are becoming increasingly—not less—concentrated on the bottom of the job ladder. As a con-

sequence full-time women workers today earn on the average only 60 percent of what men earn, and that wage gap has been increasing over the past twenty-five years in every major industry group.[1]

Not only do women work just as hard as men for less money, but they also take on more than their share of duties in the home. A woman—whether she has a full-time job or not—is expected to care for the children and do all of the cooking and cleaning. Even supposedly sensitive men who offer to "help out" with the housework unconsciously reveal their assumption that housework is the woman's job to begin with.

In today's society, if a man earns a good living, his wife is obliged to abandon her own career aspirations to stay at home with the children. Not surprisingly, the great majority of these housewives—particularly those who are educated—are bored, depressed, and frustrated by a lifestyle that affords them no independence or intellectual stimulation. One woman, quoted by Betty Friedan in her 1963 book *The Feminine Mystique*, says, "I . . . feel I have no personality. I'm a server of food and putter-on of pants and a bedmaker, somebody who can be called on when you want something. But who am I?"[2]

## A Woman's Identity as Her Sexual Role

Single working women, housewives, and working women with families face different challenges, but their problems stem from one source: the assumption that a woman's identity is based on her sexual role. In the home, a woman is expected to be the domestic servant, cook, and child care provider. With men, she is judged more on her appearance than on the quality of her opinions. Even in the workplace, women are limited by their gender, slated for "female" jobs such as secretarial work rather than higher-paying, more intellectually challenging "male" jobs such as executive positions. To find clear evidence of this, one need only look at the Sunday newspaper, which segregates its employment ads according to gender.

Therefore, a woman is always perceived in terms of her femininity. She is given no opportunity to express the various other qualities she may possess, such as intelligence, ambition, or business acuity. Viewed mainly as a wife, mother, daughter, and sex object, she is defined by her relationships with men. According to one feminist group, women

> are authentic, legitimate, real to the extent that we are the property of some man whose name we bear. To be a woman who belongs to no man is to be invisible, pathetic, inauthentic, unreal. He confirms our image of us—of what we have to be in order to be acceptable by him—but not our real selves; he confirms our womanhood—as he defines it, in relation to him—but cannot confirm our personhood, our selves as absolutes. As long as we are dependent on the male culture for this definition, for this approval, we cannot be free.[3]

## A Fundamental Reevaluation of Roles

The women's liberation movement is an essential step toward affirming women's identity as individuals. Its main goal is to break down the social conventions that dictate what women's—and men's—roles should be. As women's liberation movement member Mary C. Segers claims, "What is now required is a fundamental re-evaluation of what it means to be a woman—*and* what it means to be a man. Traditional stereotypes of masculinity and femininity have outlived their usefulness. Women and men are persons, not sex objects and breadwinners. No individual of either sex should feel constrained by social conventions and role conceptions to do only certain things and not others."[4]

Because the women's liberation movement aims to reform roles for both sexes, it will improve society for men as well as women. One major benefit will be romantic relationships that are more honest and satisfying. As feminist Gloria Steinem explains,

If role reform sounds sexually unsettling, think how it will change the sexual hypocrisy we have now. No more sex arranged on the barter system, with women pretending interest, and men never sure whether they are loved for themselves or for the security few women can get any other way. . . . No more men who are encouraged to spend a lifetime living with inferiors; with housekeepers, or dependent creatures who are still children. No more domineering wives, emasculating women, and "Jewish mothers," all of whom are simply human beings with all their normal ambition and drive confined to the home. No more unequal partnerships that eventually doom love and sex.[5]

In addition, although women's liberation entails that men relinquish their entitlement to domination, it will also free them from their own rigid societal roles. Just as women will not be entirely responsible for housework and child care, men will not be expected to be the only means of support for a family. This does not mean that roles will be reversed, with women taking over the workplace and men restricted to the domestic arena. Women's liberation is not about women switching places with men but about creating a flexible society in which people base their life decisions solely on their goals and desires, not preestablished roles.

1. *National Organization for Women Statement of Purpose*, 1966, in Miriam Schneir, ed., *Feminism in Our Time: The Essential Writings, World War II to the Present*. New York: Vintage Books, 1994, p. 98.

2. Quoted in Betty Friedan, *The Feminine Mystique*. New York: W. W. Norton, 1963, p. 21.

3. Radicalesbians, "The Woman-Identified Woman," in Alexander Bloom and Wini Breines, eds., *"Takin' It to the Streets": A Sixties Reader*. New York: Oxford University Press, 1995, p. 518.

4. Mary C. Segers, "The New Civil Rights: Fem Lib!" *Catholic World*, August 1970, in William Dudley, ed., *The 1960s: Opposing Viewpoints*. San Diego: Greenhaven Press, 1997, p. 197.

5. Gloria Steinem, "What Would It Be Like If Women Win," 1970, in Bloom and Breines, *"Takin' It to the Streets*," p. 467.

*"The life of a woman inspired by radical feminism is one of
loneliness."*

# The Women's
# Liberation Movement
# Harms Women

In August 1968, a swarm of radical feminists paraded along
the Atlantic City boardwalk to protest the annual Miss
America Pageant. To express their belief that the image of
Miss America "oppresses women," the enraged feminists
threw bras, girdles, curlers, and issues of *Cosmopolitan* and
*Family Circle*—along with other "objects of female torture"—
into a huge "Freedom Trash Can."

These angry young women are members of the women's
liberation movement, a wave of radical feminism that is
sweeping the nation. What quarrel do these feminists have
with innocent figures such as Miss America? Quite simply,
that she represents femininity. This is the central irony of the
women's liberation movement. While it claims to support
women, the movement actually despises anything that is
uniquely feminine: grace, charm, and especially beauty. In its
utopia, women would likely don regulation overalls and work
boots.

The only thing worse than femininity, in the view of the
women's liberation movement, is men themselves, whom they
consider to be evil incarnate. One women's libber asserts that

"white males are most responsible for the destruction of human life and environment on the planet today."[1] Valerie Solanas of the militant feminist group Society for Cutting Up Men (SCUM) goes so far as to say that "[the male] is trapped in a twilight zone halfway between humans and apes, and is far worse off than the apes because, unlike the apes, he is capable of a large array of negative feelings—hate, jealousy, contempt, disgust, guilt, shame, doubt."[2] Naturally, feminists also castigate men as oppressors of women. As the Redstockings collective writes, "Men have controlled all political, economic, and cultural institutions and backed up this control with physical force. They have used their power to keep women in an inferior position. . . . *All men* have oppressed women."[3]

## The Women's Liberation Movement and Motherhood

Feminists despise men because they feel that men "force" women into their roles as mothers. This notion is ridiculous. Women are mothers because they have the ability to bear and nurse children. This is not an unfair edict set down by men; it is merely a fact of biology—one that most women view as a privilege, not a detriment. In contrast to what the women's liberation movement claims, motherhood is both individually satisfying and universally significant. As religious leader David O. McKay writes,

> This ability and willingness properly to rear children . . . make motherhood the noblest office or calling in the world. She who can paint a masterpiece or write a book that will influence millions deserves the admiration and the plaudits of mankind; but she who rears successfully a family of healthy, beautiful sons and daughters, whose influence will be felt through generations to come . . . long after paintings shall have faded, and books and statues shall have decayed . . . deserves the highest honor that man can give.[4]

Moreover, motherhood is certainly more rewarding than the tedious, day-to-day labor of men, who commonly experience ulcers and other medical problems as a result of the stresses they undergo at work. American women, on the other hand, have a style of living that, according to *Newsweek*, "women of other lands could only dream of." [5] Love, comfort, and economic security are just a few of the benefits enjoyed by a typical middle-class woman in the United States. These benefits were widely appreciated until the women's liberation movement began touting the ideology that being a wife and mother was somehow degrading.

## Women in the Workplace

No one would deny women the right to work if they wish to do so and the right to be compensated equally for equal work. However, most women do *not* do work equal to that of men. According to the 1963 report of the President's Commission on the Status of Women, employers prefer to hire men over women because "the employment pattern of younger women is in and out of the labor force, working for a time before marriage and thereafter putting family obligations first until their children are grown." [6] The report also notes that employers are frustrated with women's high rates of sickness, absenteeism, and turnover.

Women are less reliable employees than men because they must juggle an impossible assortment of responsibilities. No one could honestly expect women to hold down a demanding job while simultaneously attending to household duties and child care. As Anne Bernays explains,

> If women are willing to acknowledge the remotest obligation to husband and children, especially to children during their fragile first five or six years of life then they can't summon the time, physical energy, and psychic equipment to do two jobs simultaneously. You can't split a woman's life down the middle

and expect each half, like a severed worm, to go happily crawling off, to survive and function in perfect health.[7]

## A Life of Loneliness

The "solution" that feminism offers to this dilemma is for women to give up family entirely. There is no mistaking the women's liberation movement's antimarriage agenda. Feminist Beverly Jones claims that

> [women] must reject romanticism. Romance, like the rabbit of the dog track, is the illusive, fake, and never-attained reward which for the benefit and amusement of our masters keeps us running and thinking in safe circles. A relationship between a man and a woman is no more or less personal a relationship than is the relationship between a woman and her maid, a master and slave, a teacher and his student.[8]

By indoctrinating women with the belief that marriage is inherently oppressive, the women's liberation movement prepares them for an existence devoid of love, romantic intimacy, and children. The life of a woman inspired by radical feminism is one of loneliness. If the movement were really dedicated to helping women, it would not advocate such a destructive philosophy. However, women's liberation is clearly more concerned with taking revenge on men for some perceived injustice than with promoting the interests of real-life women.

1. Robin Morgan, "Goodbye to All That," February 1970, in Miriam Schneir, ed., *Feminism in Our Time: The Essential Writings, World War II to the Present*. New York: Vintage Books, 1994, p. 150.
2. Valerie Solanas, "The SCUM Manifesto," *PHOENIX PRESS*, 1968. www.ai.mit.edu/~shivers/rants/scum.html.

3. Shulamith Firestone and Ellen Willis, "Redstockings Manifesto," February 1970, in Schneir, *Feminism in Our Time*, p. 127.

4. David O. McKay, "On Motherhood," 1936. www.xmission.com/~dkenison/lds/gtp/arc/dom_moth.html.

5. *Newsweek*, March 7, 1960, quoted in Betty Friedan, *The Feminine Mystique*. New York: W. W. Norton, 1963, p. 24.

6. *American Women*, the report of the President's Commission on the Status of Women, 1963, in Schneir, *Feminism in Our Time*, p. 45.

7. Anne Bernays, "What Are You Supposed to Do If You Like Children?" *Atlantic Monthly*, 1970, in William Dudley, ed., *The 1960s: Opposing Viewpoints*. San Diego: Greenhaven Press, 1997, p. 209.

8. Beverly Jones, "The Manifesto," 1967, in Schneir, *Feminism in Our Time*, pp. 119–20.

## CHAPTER 3

# How Has the Sixties Influenced Contemporary Society?

*"The Great Society created a humanistic government, one that took direct action to remedy the problems of its citizens."*

# The Great Society Has Benefited America

On November 22, 1963, President John F. Kennedy was assassinated in Dallas, Texas, a tragic event that suddenly catapulted Lyndon B. Johnson to the presidency. Less than two hours after Kennedy was pronounced dead, Johnson took the oath of office and assured the grieving country that he would carry out Kennedy's policies.

At the top of Johnson's agenda was to enact Kennedy's civil rights bill. In 1964, Johnson signed the Civil Rights Act, a sweeping ban of racial segregation and discrimination in public accommodations. Johnson's success in the realm of civil rights, as well as his general support for Kennedy's policies, helped him achieve a landslide victory over conservative Republican Barry Goldwater in the presidential election of 1964.

This victory was clear testimony to the nation's spirit of liberalism. At the time, the civil rights, women's liberation, and other movements for social change were creating widespread awareness of the inequalities present in American society—in particular, racial discrimination and poverty. Johnson pledged to ameliorate these problems with a plan of government he called the "Great Society." In a 1964 speech, he described the Great Society as a nation that

> rests on abundance and liberty for all. It demands an end to poverty and racial injustice. . . . The Great Society is a place where every child can find knowledge to enrich his mind and to enlarge his talents.[1]

## A Noble Vision

As his first steps toward fulfilling this vision, Johnson increased federal aid for education, urban renewal, and environmental protection. He established Medicaid and Medicare, programs that guaranteed the poor and elderly access to health care. He launched a vigorous "War on Poverty"—a combination of unemployment compensation, expanded welfare benefits, job training, low-income housing,

*Vice President Lyndon B. Johnson takes the oath of office aboard Air Force One just hours after President John F. Kennedy was pronounced dead.*

and educational programs. He also created arts programs such as the National Endowment for the Arts and the Public Broadcasting System.

The Great Society strove to accomplish something that had never been attempted before in American society: the assurance that every member of society, regardless of race, income level, or age, would have equal access to food, shelter, health care, education, and job training. In short, the Great Society created a humanistic government, one that took direct action to remedy the problems of its citizens.

Although the large majority of Americans supported the Great Society, Johnson's success in the domestic arena was overshadowed by his unpopular policies in Vietnam. However, although Johnson may have failed in his attempts to conclude the war in Vietnam, he left a noble and admirable legacy in the Great Society.

## The Advancement of Social Justice

There are a number of ways in which Great Society programs have benefited—and continue to benefit—Americans. Probably the most important development was the advancement of social justice. Johnson implemented three pieces of legislation that directly affected the lives of blacks and other disadvantaged Americans. First, the Civil Rights Act of 1964 made racial segregation and discrimination a serious crime. It also gave the federal government the authority to intervene if individual states failed to support the statute, a provision that helped safeguard the rights of blacks living in southern states.

Second, Johnson's Voting Rights Act of 1965 ensured black Americans their right to vote. Prior to the passage of this law, racist local governments in the South had prevented blacks from voting by requiring that they pass difficult examinations—ostensibly given for the purpose of determining literacy—in order to be allowed to vote. The Voting Rights Act made these tests illegal and asserted that a sixth grade education was sufficient proof of literacy.

The third program that Johnson developed in the cause of social justice was affirmative action. In an executive order given in 1965, Johnson expanded opportunities within the workplace by ruling that employers must actively seek out blacks, other minorities, and women when hiring. In explaining why affirmative action was so essential for black Americans, Johnson said,

> You do not wipe away the scar of centuries by saying: Now you are free to go where you want, do as you desire, and choose the leaders you please. You do not take a person who, for years, has been hobbled by chains and liberate him, bring him up to the starting line of a race and then say, "You are free to compete with all the others," and still justly believe that you have been completely fair.[2]

## Improved Access to Health Care

In addition to improving the lives of black Americans, the Great Society also helped the elderly through the enactment of Medicare, which guaranteed affordable health care to all Americans over the age of sixty-five. Before Medicare was passed in 1965, most elderly Americans found themselves without health insurance after retirement, and they faced the constant worry of how to pay their exorbitant medical bills. With the passage of Medicare, the elderly no longer had to postpone or forgo health care for fear of financial destitution. Karen Davis, reporting on the success of Medicare before the U.S. House of Representatives Committee on Ways and Means in 1995, cites that "Medicare serves 37 million Americans; three-fourths of whom have incomes below $25,000, and only 5% of whom have incomes exceeding $50,000. Medicare has improved access to care and contributed to better health outcomes for millions of elderly Americans."[3]

## The War on Poverty

Medicaid, a program similar to Medicare, provided affordable health care for the poor. Medicaid was part of Johnson's War on Poverty, a plan designed to help those living in extreme poverty. In the 1960s, the country appeared on the surface to be affluent, but in reality, one-fifth of all Americans were poor. Johnson himself had been poor, having grown up in a small cabin in rural Texas, and knew firsthand the difficulty of climbing out of poverty. He believed that most of the poor could improve their situation if only the government would provide them with a minimal amount of assistance.

Therefore, Johnson's War on Poverty attacked poverty on two fronts. First, it provided the poor with a basic level of subsistence by guaranteeing access to health care through Medicaid, affordable housing, and cash assistance. Second, it gave people the chance to improve their skills and education through programs such as the Job Corps, which provided vocational training, and Head Start, which prepared disadvantaged preschool students to succeed in grade school. These programs provided opportunities for the poor to obtain challenging jobs and careers.

In this way, the War on Poverty has been able to drastically reduce the number of people living in poverty. As Steve Kangas writes, "Johnson's Great Society reduced [poverty from 20 percent in the 1950s] to 11.1 percent by 1973."[4] Furthermore, an analysis of census data by Wendell E. Primus, in conjunction with the Center on Budget and Policy Priorities, found that "In 1995, [government] safety net programs cut poverty nearly in half."[5]

## The Conservative Attack on the Great Society

Despite the Great Society's obvious successes, conservatives want to completely cut all social programs, eliminating everything from *Sesame Street* on public television to vital medical care for the elderly.

Many of their criticisms of social programs stem from their belief that the government should have no role in eradicating the social and economic inequities of society. However, without action on the part of the government, the opportunities of many Americans will remain limited. For example, children who are born into poverty usually live in high-crime neighborhoods and attend low-quality schools, and therefore they do not acquire the education, skills, and social networks necessary for success. This often puts them at a disadvantage for life. It is unrealistic to think that, in the face of these deeply entrenched inequalities, people can just "pull themselves up by their bootstraps."

The solution is not to ignore these inequalities or to merely support the poor with cash handouts. Instead, it is the government's moral duty to remedy social inequities by providing the poor and otherwise disadvantaged with the opportunities they need to succeed. The Great Society has provided many of these desperately needed opportunities and, in doing so, has helped to create a society that can truly be called a democracy.

1. Lyndon B. Johnson, "Great Society Speech," 1964, *Public Papers of the Presidents of the United States, Book I (1963-64)*. http://hs1.hst.msu.edu/~hst306/documents/great.html.

2. Lyndon B. Johnson, "To Fulfill These Rights." http://userwww.sfsu.edu/~mmartin/sunsh.htm.

3. Karen Davis, "Medicare Budgetary Savings: Implications for Beneficiaries," statement before the U.S. House of Representatives Committee on Ways and Means hearing on Medicare, September 22, 1995. http://cpn.org/library/cotext.html

4. Steve Kangas, "Myth: Welfare Increases Poverty." www.scruz.net/~kangaroo/L-welfare poverty.htm.

5. *Center on Budget and Policy Priorities*, "Government Benefit Programs Cut Poverty Nearly in Half Last Year, Setting a Record for Poverty Reduction," October 9, 1996, p. 1. www.cbpp.org/prsfnt.htm.

*"The Great Society completely undermines one of the guiding principles of American society: the belief that people must take personal responsibility for their successes or failures."*

# The Great Society Has Been a Failure

The 1960s has changed America in a variety of ways, but its most distinct and most damaging legacy has been the Great Society, a plan of government developed by President Lyndon B. Johnson in the years between 1964 and 1968. This plan had, at first, the noble goal of eliminating racial segregation and discrimination. To that end, Johnson signed the Civil Rights Act of 1964 and the Voting Rights Act of 1965, laws that were instrumental in guaranteeing black Americans equal access to public accommodations and voting.

However, Johnson was not satisfied with these reforms. His ego inflated by his landslide victory in the presidential election of 1964, Johnson believed that the public had given him license to reinvent government according to his own views—and this is exactly what he did. He allocated massive amounts of federal funds—taxpayers' money, that is—to create a variety of social programs, most of them aimed at helping the poor or other groups supposedly in need of assistance. These programs included unemployment compensation, subsidized housing and health care for the poor, increased welfare benefits, and Medicare, a costly health insurance plan for the elderly. In addition, under the Great Society's National Endowment for the Arts, the government saw fit to subsidize the careers of private artists and writers. In fact, the only people *not* subsidized under Johnson's Great Society were responsible, hardworking citizens.

## The Era of Big Government

The Great Society instituted the era of "big government" in America—an era that still plagues the country today. Big government is widely supported by liberals, who falsely presume that only the government—rather than individuals or private charities—can solve society's problems. However, big government means essentially one thing: high taxes. The inevitable consequence of Johnson's expensive social programs has been a dramatic rise in taxes. After three decades of the Great Society, federal, state, and local taxes combined eat up 40 percent of the average citizen's paycheck.

Not only do high taxes place a severe financial burden on working Americans, but they also constitute an abuse of power. The government should not be allowed, as it is doing now, to dictate how its citizens should spend their money. This infringes on people's most basic right: the right to choose what to do with their own possessions.

## An Involuntary Health Care Program

This is the main problem with Medicare, a Great Society program intended to provide affordable health insurance to the elderly. Medicare *forces* all working adults to pay a portion of their income to a fund that will presumably finance their health care once they reach the age of sixty-five. However, it is unlikely that this will happen, because Medicare is going broke. According to policy analysts John C. Liu and Robert E. Moffit, Medicare "will be insolvent by 2002"[1] unless taxpayers are encumbered with an enormous tax hike.

There is a reason why Medicare is financially doomed. Since the government picks up the tab for the health care of all Medicare beneficiaries, there is no incentive for patients, doctors, and hospitals to keep costs down. Writer John McCay explains:

> Think of what happens when you go to a party and the host says, "The food is free, take what you want." What do most people do? They gorge; they fill their plates and stuff their mouths; they wrap up some more to take home. Why not? The food's free. It's the same with free medical care. That's why the cost for Medicare . . . has exploded since 1965.[2]

## The Failed War on Poverty

While Medicare is clearly wasteful, the most destructive of all Great Society programs are those that purport to help the poor.

Aiding the poor is a noble and important endeavor. Private charities are in existence for that very purpose, and many Americans contribute liberally to such institutions. It is a different matter altogether when the government *compels* people to help the poor. In a free society, this is unacceptable.

Moreover, government handouts don't help the poor at all. Ironically, the War on Poverty has actually aggravated the problems it was intended to solve. Kenneth Whyte notes that, between 1965 and 1980, the period when Great Society expenditures were highest,

> the percentage of Americans living in poverty was unchanged at thirteen percent. . . . School-enrollment levels had failed to improve, and the quality of education in the U.S. began to plummet. The number of welfare cases had doubled. Youth unemployment had increased, despite relatively strong economic growth. The divorce and illegitimacy rates had shot up, especially among the poor.[3]

The millions of dollars thrown into Johnson's War on

Poverty program over the course of three decades have done nothing to alter the poverty rate in America. According to member of Congress Dick Armey, "Although the poverty rate has remained relatively steady since 1965, welfare spending has risen from 1.5 percent of gross national product when Lyndon Johnson launched [the War on Poverty] in 1965 to 5 percent today."[4]

## Behavioral Poverty

Not only has the Great Society failed to alleviate poverty, but it has also made life worse for the poor. These programs have led to a drastic increase in what Armey calls "behavioral poverty—dependency, lack of educational aspiration and achievement, increased single parenthood and illegitimacy."[5] The reason for this is simple. The Great Society completely undermines one of the guiding principles of American society: the belief that people must take personal responsibility for their successes or failures.

Once people recognize that they can get whatever they need for free—be it food, housing, health care, or simply money—the incentive to work becomes obsolete. Why work eight hours a day at a low-wage job when welfare brings in the same amount of money? As Dean Koontz, writer and former Great Society worker, says, "When the safety net becomes a steel mesh that you're never going to fall through, then there's almost no motivation for a lot of people."[6] Instead of reducing poverty, welfare actually gives poor people an economic incentive to stay poor.

## Incentives for Single Motherhood and Illegitimacy

Just as Great Society antipoverty programs completely eradicate work incentives, they also create strong economic incentives for single motherhood and illegitimacy. Since the inception of the Great Society's War on Poverty in 1965, the illegitimacy rate among black Americans has risen from 25 percent to 66 percent in 1994, and it shows no sign of slowing. This is due mostly to the perverse incentives of Aid to Families with Dependent Children (AFDC). AFDC, developed in 1935 by President Franklin D. Roosevelt, was originally intended to provide financial support to mothers who were widowed and destitute. However, under Johnson's War on Poverty, AFDC was handed out freely to all poor single women with children, until 1996, when legislators eradicated the program, acknowledging its failure. The program, by providing welfare benefits only to single mothers, "transformed marriage from a legal institution that protects and nurtures children into an institution that financially penalizes nearly all low-income parents who choose it,"[7] in Armey's words. Furthermore, since welfare beneficiaries receive more money for each child they have, it is no surprise that out-of-wedlock births have skyrocketed over the last three decades.

Illegitimate children almost always live in single-parent households, and because of this, they often face emotional and social problems. As Jean Bethke Elshtain maintains,

> A high correlation exists between broken homes and a whole range of troubles for children. Three out of four teenage suicides occur in households where a parent is absent. Eighty percent of adolescents in psychiatric hospitals come from broken homes. Tracking studies report that five out of six adolescents caught up in the criminal-justice system come from families where a parent (usually the father) is absent.[8]

## Perpetuating the Cycle of Dependence

The types of problems that children of single mothers are prone to, such as juvenile violence, low educational achievement, and poverty, also make them extremely likely to become dependent on government assistance once they are adults. Welfare dependency becomes a self-perpetuating cycle, with parents passing dependency along to their kids like an inheritance.

Thus, instead of a safety net, the public dole has become a way of life—one that no longer carries a negative stigma. Whereas welfare dependency was once avoided because it was considered shameful, now entire communities are dependent on some type of government assistance, from food stamps to subsidized housing. As a result, the poor have begun to accept welfare as a normal aspect of life. The more "normal" welfare dependency becomes, the more likely people are to feel entitled to government assistance. Myron Magnet, editor of Manhattan's *City Journal*, writes that federal assistance has "created a class of minorities [who] believed that they were victims, justified in an adversary relation to America, entitled to welfare, not responsible for their actions, and doing right to be promiscuous or to produce children out of wedlock."[9]

Within the field of education, it is a commonly accepted truth that low expectations tend to encourage poor results. The same applies to society as a whole. If the government continues to disempower poor people by telling them they are incapable of succeeding, it becomes virtually inevitable that they will not. In contrast, if the government gives people the opportunity to take responsibility for their actions, they will rise to the occasion. Therefore, the first step toward ending America's poverty is to put an immediate halt to Great Society programs.

The failure of the Great Society's antipoverty programs exemplifies big government's central fallacy: that people need the government to alleviate their problems. When the government eliminates incentives for people to address their own problems, it inevitably creates more problems than it can possibly solve. It has taken America over thirty years to learn this painful lesson. Before any more harm is done, it is time for the Great Society, and the era of big government, to end.

1. John C. Liu and Robert E. Moffit, "A Taxpayer's Guide to the Medicare Crisis," *The Heritage Foundation Talking Points No. 10*, September 27, 1995. www.heritage.org/library/categories/healthwel/tp10.html.

2. Quoted in Jim Powell, "A Passionate Moral Attack on Government Intervention," *Laissez Faire Books*, April 1996. http://laissezfaire.org/py6996.html.

3. Kenneth Whyte, "Allan Rock," *Saturday Night*, November 1995, p. 18.

4. Dick Armey, "Public Welfare in America," *Journal of Social, Political & Economic Studies*, Summer 1994, p. 245.

5. Armey, "Public Welfare in America," p. 246.

6. Dean Koontz, interviewed by Nick Gillespie and Lisa Snell, "Contemplating Evil," *Reason*, November 1996, p. 47.

7. Armey, "Public Welfare in America," p. 246.

8. Jean Bethke Elshtain, "The Family in Trouble: Why We Should Worry," *National Forum*, Winter 1995, p. 25.

9. Myron Magnet, "The National Prospect," *Commentary*, November 1995, p. 84.

*"The activism of the sixties was directly responsible for the increased social awareness and moral consciousness that characterize American society today."*

# The Sixties Had a Positive Impact on American Values

The sixties was undoubtedly one of the most turbulent periods in American history. Within the span of five years, four respected American leaders—President John F. Kennedy, Malcolm X, Martin Luther King Jr., and Robert F. Kennedy—were assassinated. Riots erupted in many of the nation's largest cities. Civil rights protesters faced barbaric mobs of racists. Confrontations between antiwar protesters and the police often turned violent. In Vietnam, hundreds of American men, along with hundreds of Vietnamese citizens, were killed each week. To many Americans, the country seemed to be disintegrating into chaos.

However, accompanying this sense of disillusionment was a fervent desire to make society better. The crises of the sixties caused American citizens to collectively challenge the values of their country. Youth activism exposed many of these values as unethical and, in doing so, helped to change the attitudes of society as a whole. The activism of the sixties was directly responsible for the increased social awareness and moral consciousness that characterize American society today.

## Civil Rights

The most dramatic shift in attitudes has come in the area of civil rights. Before the civil rights movement, racial segregation was law in the South, and often unwritten law in the rest of the country. Racial prejudice was such that many whites did not want to live, work, or send their children to school with blacks.

The civil rights movement, by bringing the issue of racial justice into the public eye, demonstrated to America that racial prejudice was unacceptable—not only from a legal standpoint but also from a moral one. Although the movement aimed to eradicate racist laws and policies, its primary concern was to create a more loving and tolerant society. The widespread appeal of this vision made the civil rights movement a powerful force for change. As sixties' scholar Edward P. Morgan writes, "The civil rights movement derived much of its persuasive power from a moral vision of politics based on love."[1]

*The civil rights movement of the 1960s made it possible for blacks to attend formerly all-white schools and universities.*

Today, the majority of Americans believe that racism is immoral. Those who do espouse racist beliefs are typically social outcasts or members of fringe hate groups. This is a vast difference from the 1960s, when racism was often a source of pride and power. Not only did government officials throughout the South conduct racist policies, but many also went on public record justifying segregation and other forms of discrimination. For example in a televised speech in 1957, the governor of Arkansas, Orval Faubus, announced his plan to prevent black students from attending their local public school. These days, blatant racism on the part of a public official would not be tolerated. Moreover, although the subject of race still generates conflict, the vast majority of Americans agree that racism is wrong. As William R. Wineke says,

> No one in any real position of authority would ever justify racial discrimination today—not publicly and, for the most part, not privately. We have not only changed our laws, we have changed our individual attitudes. This doesn't mean we have, as a society, solved all of our racial problems. But today we are arguing about how best to achieve full equality, not about whether equality is desirable.[2]

## Women's Liberation

A similar transformation has taken place in societal attitudes toward women. Prior to the women's liberation movement of the 1960s, women's options were severely restricted. Middle-class women were sent to college mainly so that they could find a husband, and once this goal was achieved, they were expected to abandon their intellectual interests or careers in order to raise children. Those women who worked for financial reasons received less money than men for the same work and, regardless of their abilities, were not considered eligible for jobs that offered growth opportunities or high pay. Women were simply not considered to be equal to men, particularly within the workplace.

The women's liberation movement marked the first time that Americans directly challenged these assumptions about women's roles. On a practical level, the movement abolished the discriminatory policies—different pay scales for men and women, for example—that limited women's opportunities. However, as with the civil rights movement, the women's liberation movement's most profound effect was a change in attitudes. By the 1980s, "a majority of citizens agreed that men and women should share housework and child-rearing equally"[3]—a huge shift from the 1950s, when women were expected to fulfill these duties alone. Women's entries into positions previously held only by men, such as the CEO of a major company, have been made possible by the societal belief that women's roles are not confined to the home. The idea that women should have the right to pursue their own ambitions, considered to be an extremely radical concept in 1960, is now something that most people take for granted.

## The Antiwar Movement

Although the civil rights and women's liberation movements were both powerful influences on American society, perhaps the most visible movement of the 1960s was the antiwar movement. For the first time in history, Americans in significant numbers rallied against the government's war policies because they felt that those policies were immoral. Although some Americans had protested the Vietnam War from the beginning, accounts of American troops burning entire Vietnamese villages, bombing the Vietnamese countryside indiscriminately, and executing groups of Vietnamese women and children turned many former supporters against the war. By the decade's end, a vast majority of Americans were opposed to the war, and many actively protested it.

In doing so, protesters set a precedent for citizens to demand that the government act morally in its dealings with other countries. Because of the antiwar movement, Americans are no longer willing to blindly accept the government's foreign policies, especially when those policies involve war. Today, the citizens of this nation require the government to justify its actions. Writer Terry H. Anderson contends that "the sixties killed the Imperial Presidency. The commander-in-chief since has not had the power to order U.S. troops to fight in foreign lands without citizens asking, Why?"[4]

## Giving a Voice to America's Victims

Furthermore, antiwar protesters, in speaking out on behalf of the Vietnamese peasants whose land and livelihood was destroyed by American bombs and herbicides, called attention to the plight of America's victims.

All of the movements of the sixties were united by this desire to give a voice to the people who suffered oppression or discrimination as a result of American policies. Morgan explains that

> Sixties movements expressed the voices of those whom society had systematically treated as "other"— black Americans, Latinos, the poor, Native Americans, women, gays, Vietnamese peasants, . . . [and] nature. . . . In place of domination, the Movement sought community and celebrated . . . the union of equals.[5]

Therefore, the sixties created a vision of a truly moral society, a society in which all people, regardless of race, gender, or class, were equals. It demanded that America reevaluate its treatment of its disadvantaged citizens, as well as its treatment of the land itself, which was becoming increasingly ruined by human disregard. The movements of the sixties have instilled in Americans the belief that society has a duty to remedy and prevent social and environmental injustices. As William R. Garrett illustrates,

That students enter colleges and universities today with a potent belief in equality and a firm commitment to fairness is to a large extent a testament to the success of the sixties generation in promoting the recognition that no one can be rightfully excluded from, or their privileges limited in, the global community. . . . The premise was firmly institutionalized that no one should be denied full participation in the various domains of social life on the basis of such ascribed characteristics as race, ethnicity, gender, national origin [and] sexual orientation.[6]

This is not to say that America is free of moral conflict or that it has been successful in its attempts to achieve equality. The sixties has, however, brought controversy to the forefront of American society. By challenging the conventions of the status quo, sixties' activists have provoked open debate about American values—a debate that, as Anderson writes, "involves the political and the personal, and . . . asks the central question of this democracy: What is the meaning of 'America'?"[7]

1. Edward P. Morgan, *The Sixties Experience*, 1991, in William Dudley, ed., *The 1960s: Opposing Viewpoints*. San Diego: Greenhaven Press, 1997, p. 222.

2. William R. Wineke, "Slip on Those Rose-Colored Glasses for Just a Moment," *Wisconsin State Journal*, April 25, 1998, p. 1C.

3. Terry H. Anderson, *The Movement and the Sixties*. New York: Oxford University Press, 1995, p. 419.

4. Anderson, *The Movement and the Sixties*, p. 418.

5. Morgan, *The Sixties Experience*, in Dudley, *The 1960s: Opposing Viewpoints*, p. 224.

6. William R. Garrett, "Cultural Revolution and Character Formation," *World & I*, May 1998, pp. 305–306.

7. Anderson, *The Movement and the Sixties*, p. 423.

*"The new sexual norms of America have helped to destroy the institution of marriage—the one institution that provides economic and social stability for children."*

# The Sixties Had a Negative Impact on American Values

Today, most people would agree that the American society is in trouble. Since the 1960s, the rate of divorce has nearly tripled and continues to rise, with experts predicting that half of all new marriages will end in divorce. In the United States, half of all children witness the breakup of a parent's marriage; a third are born out of wedlock. The collapse of the stable, two-parent family has given rise to innumerable societal problems, including poverty, crime, teen pregnancy, and juvenile delinquency of all types.

Such a dramatic decline in values did not spring out of nowhere but can be easily traced back to the youth rebellion of the 1960s. This spirit of rebellion had its roots in important causes such as civil rights for blacks and the equal treatment of women in the workplace. However, for many teenagers, these justified forms of protest quickly degenerated into unreasoned attacks on all forms of authority. Eventually, even middle-class teenagers, antiwar radicals, and drug users felt they were the victims of an "oppressive" society. The impact of this indiscriminate rebelliousness was to degrade all American institutions and traditions, particularly the family.

## The Sexual Revolution

The so-called sexual revolution was the worst example of youth rebellion taken to the extreme. During the mid-1960s, hippies, feminists, and other rebellious youth, eager to defy adult conventions, condemned marriage as repressive, and used that ideology as an excuse to engage in promiscuous sex.

The birth control pill, which appeared on the American market in 1960, provided the practical means for this depraved behavior to flourish. By 1961, 1.2 million women were using the pill; by 1965, this number had more than quadrupled. Because the pill made sex worry-free in terms of pregnancy, women were increasingly expected to engage in premarital sex. Those who refused sex were scorned as "prudish" and risked being rejected in favor of a more "sexually liberated" woman. George A. Akerloff and Janet A. Yellen explain that "women feared, correctly, that if they refused sex-

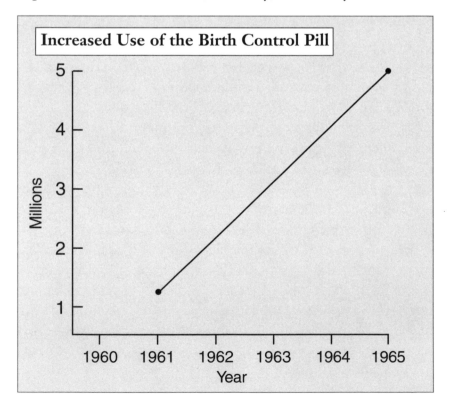

ual relations, they risked losing their partners. Sexual activity without commitment was increasingly expected in premarital relationships."[1]

The pressure for women to engage in premarital sex did not just come from men. The ideology of the sexual revolution was that "free love" was liberating and empowering for women. Sex was portrayed as a revolutionary act, something that was politically daring as well as individually gratifying.

However, the sexual revolution was anything but empowering for women. There was nothing more *disempowering* for a woman than the fear that she would be tossed aside if she did not give in to the sexual demands of men. If she did give in, she wound up feeling used and degraded when the relationship ended. Writer Roger Scruton observes that "sexual liberation . . . jeopardized everything that gives a woman confidence in her sexual feelings: love, commitment, marriage, and the family."[2]

## Promiscuity as a Cultural Norm

After more than three decades of the sexual revolution, lascivious behavior has become the norm in American society. Sadly, women today are accustomed to the expectation that they will engage in casual sex. They know full well that to resist sex is to endanger a relationship. The new value that seems to guide all sexual relationships is "anything goes."

In essence, as Elizabeth Fox-Genovese contends, the sexual revolution "permanently sever[ed] the link between sex and morality, making it increasingly difficult to censor any behavior at all."[3] Sex is no longer a sacred act of love between two committed partners but a pleasurable encounter devoid of moral significance. Because of this, all acts of sex are considered to be morally equal. As Scruton explains, "The man who has 365 partners a year, all of them strangers, is not for that reason more wicked than the man who confines his attentions to his wife, whom he loves. For, in liberated eyes, they are doing the same thing."[4]

## The Demise of Marriage

The new sexual norms of America have helped to destroy the institution of marriage—the one institution that provides economic and social stability for children. Extensive research demonstrates the importance of a two-parent family, as well as the negative effects of divorce and single-parent families. Social scientist Nicholas Zill reports that, regardless of economic circumstances, children of divorced parents are twice as likely as others to have poor relationships with their parents, drop out of high school, and experience psychological problems. Other studies have shown that children in single-parent families are more inclined to abuse drugs or get in trouble with the law. Statistics such as these are no surprise. Common sense dictates that a child who does not receive the love, supervision, and financial support of two parents begins life at a disadvantage.

America's widespread tolerance of sexual promiscuity essentially ruins this source of support for children. With no moral code guiding sexual behavior, there is nothing to prevent people from engaging in premarital or extramarital sex. Because of this, many people resist marriage altogether, choosing instead to drift in and out of sexual relationships or to cohabit with partners. As of 1996, nearly 3.7 million American households are composed of unmarried couples. Moreover, those who do marry are prone to divorce, partly because adultery has become commonplace.

Furthermore, cultural norms no longer encourage people to marry in the event of an unplanned pregnancy. Before the advent of the pill and the ensuing sexual revolution, if a man got his girlfriend pregnant, he would do the honorable thing and marry her. Social norms mandated that this was the respectable and appropriate thing to do. However, the pill led men to expect that it was the woman's responsibility not to become pregnant. Because of this mind-set, men were far less likely to marry their pregnant girlfriends. The rate of shotgun marriages—women who married as the result of an unplanned pregnancy—declined from 42 percent in 1965 to 26 percent in 1984. Rampant promiscuity only made this trend worse. Since it was common for both men and women to have multiple sexual partners, all a man had to do to get out of marrying his pregnant partner was to question whether he was truly the child's father.

As a result of this phenomenon, men today are not willing to take responsibility for an unplanned pregnancy, at least not in terms of marriage. Akerloff and Yellen explain:

> "If [a woman] is not willing to have an abortion or use contraception," the man can reason, "why should I sacrifice myself to get married?" By making the birth of the child the physical choice of the mother, the sexual revolution has made marriage and child support a social choice of the father.[5]

## A Lethal Revolution

While promiscuity has always been a bad thing, especially in terms of family stability, today it is lethal. During the 1960s, people could have sex with abandon and at least not worry about the effects on their personal health. Now, with the advent of AIDS, those who are sexually promiscuous risk death. The sixties left American society with a legacy of sexual recklessness that, in light of AIDS, is doubly destructive. This is why author Linda Ellerbee rightly states that "of all the revolutions that were started in the '60s, [the sexual revolution] probably was the most dangerous, emotionally and physically."[6]

## The Sixties and Political Correctness

While the sexual revolution was perhaps the most harmful of all activist movements, youth activism as a whole has had negative effects. It has created a society so eager to be tolerant that it refuses to make any moral judgments. Jonathan Alter contends that "we . . . feel uncomfortable passing judgment on illegitimacy, adultery and promiscuity."[7] The sixties culture replaced valid moral taboos—against premarital sex, drug use, juvenile delinquency, and a defiance of authority—with the new taboo of "political correctness," a mandate against any speech or behavior that might be considered offensive to others. In the new, liberated America, it is perfectly acceptable to engage in promiscuous behavior but unacceptable to criticize premarital sex, abortion, adultery, or even pornography. The only people not tolerated in America are those who refuse to accept this backward view of morality.

1. George A. Akerloff and Janet A. Yellen, "New Mothers, Not Married: Technology Shock, the Demise of the Shotgun Marriage, and the Increase in Out-of-Wedlock Births," *Brookings Review*, Fall 1996, p. 2.

2. Roger Scruton, "The Sex Files," *National Review*, October 12, 1998, p. 49.

3. Elizabeth Fox-Genovese, "The National Prospect," *Commentary*, November 1995, p. 53.

4. Scruton, "The Sex Files," p. 49.

5. Akerloff and Yellen, "New Mothers, Not Married," p. 2.

6. Linda Ellerbee, "The Sexual Revolution: Well, It Seemed Like a Good Idea at the Time . . .," *New Choices*, April 8, 1998, p. 38.

7. Jonathan Alter, "In the Time of Tolerance," *Newsweek*, March 30, 1998, p. 29.

# STUDY QUESTIONS

## Chapter 1

1. Viewpoint 1 argues that the Vietnam War helps to protect the welfare of South Vietnam. Viewpoint 2, in contrast, contends that the Vietnam War harms South Vietnam. Which perspective do you find more convincing and why?

2. How do Viewpoints 1 and 2 differ in their opinion of antiwar protesters?

3. According to Viewpoint 3, what social rules and taboos are hippies rebelling against? What evidence can you find that Viewpoint 4 supports these taboos?

4. From the perspective of Viewpoint 3, what motivates hippies to live the way they do? What does Viewpoint 4 regard as the primary motives of hippies?

## Chapter 2

1. What is the basic philosophy of the civil rights movement? For what reasons do Malcolm X and the Black Panther Party criticize this philosophy?

2. Tom Hayden asserts in Viewpoint 2 that rioting may be a necessary response to racial injustice. Based on what you have read in Viewpoint 1, how would Martin Luther King Jr. and other civil rights activists regard rioting? Which view do you find more persuasive and why?

3. What contrasting assumptions do Viewpoints 3 and 4 make about women's roles?

4. According to Viewpoint 3, how is the women's liberation movement beneficial to women? According to Viewpoint 4, how does the movement harm women?

## Chapter 3

1. Viewpoint 1 argues that the Great Society benefited America, while Viewpoint 2 argues that the program was counterproductive. Consulting Viewpoints 1 and 2, make a list of the positive and negative effects of the Great Society. Which list seems more persuasive and why? Do certain items on the lists contradict each other?

2. One of the major sources of controversy over the Great Society

is whether the federal government should play a role in alleviating poverty and other social problems. What arguments do Viewpoint 1 and Viewpoint 2 make in relation to this controversy?

3. According to Viewpoint 3, how did the activist movements of the sixties benefit society? According to Viewpoint 4, how did these movements harm society? Based on what you have read in Viewpoints 3 and 4, was the sixties' impact on society primarily positive, negative, or a combination of both? Provide reasons to support your answer.

4. Viewpoint 4 asserts that the sexual revolution contributed heavily to the decline of the two-parent family. Does this analysis seem reasonable? Why or why not?

# APPENDIX

## Excerpts from Original Documents
## Pertaining to the 1960s

### Document 1: The U.S. Government White Paper on Vietnam

*By 1965, U.S. forces were fully engaged in the Vietnam War. On February 27 of that year, the State Department published a report that attempted to explain the reasons behind American intervention. The report, entitled* Aggression from the North: The Record of North Vietnam's Campaign to Conquer South Vietnam, *provides the official rationale for U.S. involvement in Vietnam.*

South Vietnam is fighting for its life against a brutal campaign of terror and armed attack inspired, directed, supplied, and controlled by the Communist regime in Hanoi. This flagrant aggression has been going on for years, but recently the pace has quickened and the threat has now become acute.

The war in Vietnam is a new kind of war, a fact as yet poorly understood in most parts of the world. Much of the confusion that prevails in the thinking of many people, and even governments, stems from this basic misunderstanding. For in Vietnam a totally new brand of aggression has been loosed against an independent people who want to make their way in peace and freedom.

Vietnam is not another Greece, where indigenous guerrilla forces used friendly neighboring territory as a sanctuary.

Vietnam is not another Malaya, where Communist guerrillas were, for the most part, physically distinguishable from the peaceful majority they sought to control.

Vietnam is not another Philippines, where Communist guerrillas were physically separated from the source of their moral and physical support.

Above all, the war in Vietnam is not a spontaneous and local rebellion against the established government.

There are elements in the Communist program of conquest directed against South Vietnam common to each of the previous areas of aggression and subversion. But there is one fundamental difference. In Vietnam a Communist government has set out deliberately to conquer a sovereign people in a neighboring state. And to achieve its end, it has used every resource of its own government to carry out its carefully planned program of concealed aggression. North Vietnam's commitment to seize control of the South is no less total than was the commitment of the regime in North Korea in 1950. But knowing the consequences of the latter's undisguised attack, the planners in Hanoi have tried desperately to conceal their hand. They have failed and their aggression is as real as that of an invading army.

## Evidence of North Vietnamese Aggression

This report is a summary of the massive evidence of North Vietnamese aggression obtained by the Government of South Vietnam. This evidence has been jointly analyzed by South Vietnamese and American experts.

The evidence shows that the hard core of the Communist forces attacking South Vietnam were trained in the North and ordered into the South by Hanoi. It shows that the key leadership of the Vietcong (VC), the officers and much of the cadre, many of the technicians, political organizers, and propagandists have come from the North and operate under Hanoi's direction. It shows that the training of essential military personnel and their infiltration into the South is directed by the Military High Command in Hanoi. In recent months new types of weapons have been introduced in the VC army, for which all ammunition must come from outside sources. Communist China and other Communist states have been the prime suppliers of these weapons and ammunition, and they have been channeled primarily through North Vietnam.

The directing force behind the effort to conquer South Vietnam is the Communist Party in the North, the Lao Dong (Workers) Party. As in every Communist state, the party is an integral part of the regime itself. North Vietnamese officials have expressed their firm determination to absorb South Vietnam into the Communist world.

Through its Central Committee, which controls the Government of the North, the Lao Dong Party directs the total political and military effort of the Vietcong. The Military High Command in the North trains the military men and sends them into South Vietnam. The Central Research Agency, North Vietnam's central intelligence organization, directs the elaborate espionage and subversion effort . . . .

The record is conclusive. It establishes beyond question that North Vietnam is carrying out a carefully conceived plan of aggression against the South. It shows that North Vietnam has intensified its efforts in the years since it was condemned by the International Control Commission. It proves that Hanoi continues to press its systematic program of armed aggression into South Vietnam. This aggression violates the United Nations Charter. It is directly contrary to the Geneva Accords of 1954 and of 1962 to which North Vietnam is a party. It is a fundamental threat to the freedom and security of South Vietnam.

The people of South Vietnam have chosen to resist this threat. At their request, the United States has taken its place beside them in their defensive struggle.

The United States seeks no territory, no military bases, no favored position. But we have learned the meaning of aggression elsewhere in the post-war world, and we have met it.

If peace can be restored in South Vietnam, the United States will be ready at once to reduce its military involvement. But it will not abandon friends who want to remain free. It will do what must be done to help them. The choice now between peace and continued and increasingly destructive conflict is one for the authorities in Hanoi to make.

U. S. State Department, *Aggression from the North: The Record of North Vietnam's Campaign to Conquer South Vietnam*, February 27, 1965. http://wiretap.spies.com/ftp.items/Gov/US-History/Vietnam/white-paper.txt.

## Document 2: The Antiwar Movement

*As U.S. involvement in Vietnam escalated, the antiwar movement grew increasingly vocal and visible, spreading beyond the student population. By the late 1960s, religious leaders, women's groups, businesspeople, and even politicians had begun to speak out against the war. In the following selection, excerpted from an article published in the* New York Times *Magazine on August 20, 1967, Arkansas senator J. William Fulbright explains the importance of the antiwar movement. He contends that Vietnam War dissenters are upholding American values by refusing to accept that the United States is an imperial nation.*

When he visited America a hundred years ago, Thomas Huxley wrote: "I cannot say that I am in the slightest degree impressed by your bigness, or your material resources, as such. Size is not grandeur, and territory does not make a nation. The great issue, about which hangs the terror of over-hanging fate, is what are you going to do with all these things?"

The question is still with us, and we seem to have come to a time of historical crisis when its answer can no longer be deferred. Before the Second World War our world role was a potential role; we were important in the world for what we *could* do with our power, for the leadership we *might* provide, for the example we *might* set. Now the choices are almost gone: we are, almost, the world's self-appointed policeman; we are, almost, the world defender of the status quo. We are well on our way to becoming a traditional great power—an imperial nation if you will—engaged in the exercise of power for its own sake, exercising it to the limit of our capacity and beyond, filling every vacuum and extending the American "presence" to the farthest reaches of the earth. And, as with the great empires of the past, as the power grows, it is becoming an end in itself, separated except by ritual incantation from its initial motives, governed, it would seem, by its own mystique, power without philosophy or purpose.

That describes what we have *almost* become, but we have not become a traditional empire yet. The old values remain—the populism and the optimism, the individualism and the rough-hewn equality, the friendliness and the good humor, the inventiveness and the zest for life, the caring about people and the sympathy for the underdog, and the idea, which goes back to the American Revolution, that maybe—just maybe—we can set an example of democracy and human dignity for the world.

That is something which none of the great empires of the past has ever done, or tried to do, or wanted to do, but we were bold enough—or presumptuous enough—to think that we might be able to do it. And there are a great many Americans who still think we can do it, or at least they want to try.

That, I believe, is what all the hue and cry is about—the dissent in the

Senate and the protest marches in the cities, the letters to the President from the student leaders and former Peace Corps Volunteers, the lonely searching of conscience by a student facing the draft and the letter to a Senator from a soldier in the field who can no longer accept the official explanations of why he has been sent to fight in the jungles of Vietnam. All believe that their country was cut out for something more ennobling than imperial destiny. Our youth are showing that they still believe in the American dream, and their protests attest to its continuing vitality.

## American Values

There appeared in a recent issue of the journal *Foreign Affairs* a curious little article complaining about the failure of many American intellectuals to support what the author regards as America's unavoidable "imperial role" in the world. The article took my attention because it seems a faithful statement of the governing philosophy of American foreign policy while also suggesting how little the makers of that policy appreciate the significance of the issue between themselves and their critics. It is taken for granted—not set forth as a hypothesis to be proven—that any great power, in the author's words, "is entangled in a web of responsibilities from which there is no hope of escape," and that "there is no way the United States, as the world's mightiest power, can avoid such an imperial role. . . ." The author's displeasure with the "intellectuals" (he uses the word more or less to describe people who disagree with the Administration's policy) is that, in the face of this alleged historical inevitability, they are putting up a disruptive, irritating and futile resistance. They are doing this, he believes, because they are believers in "ideology"—the better word would be "values" or "ideals"—and this causes their thinking to be "irrelevant" to foreign policy.

Here, inadvertently, the writer puts his finger on the nub of the current crisis. The students and churchmen and professors who are protesting the Vietnam war do not accept the notion that foreign policy is a matter of expedients to which values are irrelevant. They reject this notion because they understand, as some of our policymakers do not understand, that it is ultimately self-defeating to "fight fire with fire," that you cannot defend your values in a manner that does violence to those values without destroying the very thing you are trying to defend. They understand, as our policymakers do not, that when American soldiers are sent, in the name of freedom, to sustain corrupt dictators in a civil war, . . . damage—perhaps irreparable damage—is being done to the very values that are meant to be defended. The critics understand, as our policymakers do not, that, through the undemocratic expedients we have adopted for the defense of American democracy, we are weakening it to a degree that is beyond the resources of our bitterest enemies.

Nor do the dissenters accept the romantic view that a nation is powerless to choose the role it will play in the world, that some mystic force of history or destiny requires a powerful nation to be an imperial nation. . . . They do not accept the view that, because other great nations have pursued power for its own sake—a pursuit which invariably has ended in decline or disaster—America must do the same. They think we have some choice about our own future and that the best basis for exercising that choice is the values on which this republic was founded. . . .

Even the most ardent advocates of an imperial role for the United States would probably agree that the proper objective of our foreign policy is the fostering of a world environment in which we can, with reasonable security, devote our main energies to the realization of the values of our own society. This does not require the adoption or imposition of these values on anybody, but it does require us so to conduct ourselves that our society does not seem hateful and repugnant to others.

At the present, much of the world is repelled by America and what America seems to stand for. Both in our foreign affairs and in our domestic life we convey an image of violence; I do not care very much about images as distinguished from the things they reflect, but this image is rooted in reality. Abroad we are engaged in a savage and unsuccessful war against poor people in a small and backward nation. At home—largely because of the neglect resulting from twenty-five years of preoccupation with foreign involvements—our cities are exploding in violent protest against generations of social injustice. America, which only a few years ago seemed to the world to be a model of democracy and social justice, has become a symbol of violence and undisciplined power. . . .

## Moral Leadership

Far from building a safe world environment for American values, our war in Vietnam and the domestic deterioration which it has aggravated are creating a most uncongenial world atmosphere for American ideas and values. The world has no need, in this age of nationalism and nuclear weapons, for a new imperial power, but there is a great need of moral leadership—by which I mean the leadership of decent example. That role could be ours but we have vacated the field, and all that has kept the Russians from filling it is their own lack of imagination.

At the same time, as we have noted, and of even greater fundamental importance, our purposeless and undisciplined use of power is causing a profound controversy in our own society. This in a way is something to be proud of. We have sickened but not succumbed, and just as a healthy body fights disease, we are fighting the alien concept which is being thrust upon us, not by history but by our policymakers in the Department of State and the Pentagon. We are proving the strength of the American dream by resisting the dream of an imperial destiny. We are demonstrating the validity of our traditional values by the difficulty we are having in betraying them.

The principal defenders of these values are our remarkable younger generation, something of whose spirit is expressed in a letter which I received from an American soldier in Vietnam. Speaking of the phony propaganda on both sides, and then of the savagery of the war, of the people he describes as the "real casualties"—"the farmers and their families in the Delta mangled by air strikes, and the villagers here killed and burned out by our friendly Korean mercenaries"—this young soldier then asks ". . . whatever has become of our dream? Where is that America that opposed tyrannies at every turn, without inquiring first whether some particular forms of tyranny might be of use to us? Of the three rights which men have, the first, as I recall, was the right to life. How, then, have we come to be killing so many in such a dubious cause?". . .

An unnecessary and immoral war deserves in its own right to be liquidated; when its effect in addition is the aggravation of grave problems and the corrosion of values in our own society, its liquidation under terms of reasonable and honorable compromise is doubly imperative. Our country is being weakened by a grotesque inversion of priorities, the effects of which are becoming clear to more and more Americans—in the Congress, in the press and in the country at large. . . .

## The Younger Generation

While the country sickens for lack of moral leadership, a most remarkable younger generation has taken up the standard of American idealism. Unlike so many of their elders, they have perceived the fraud and sham in American life and are unequivocally rejecting it. Some, the hippies, have simply withdrawn; and while we may regret the loss of their energies and their sense of decency, we can hardly gainsay their evaluation of the state of society. Others of our youth are sardonic and skeptical, not, I think, because they do not want ideals but because they want the genuine article and will not tolerate fraud. Others—students who wrestle with their consciences about the draft, soldiers who wrestle with their consciences about the war, Peace Corps Volunteers who strive to light the spark of human dignity among the poor of India or Brazil and VISTA [Volunteers in Service to America] volunteers who try to do the same for our own poor in Harlem or Appalachia—are striving to keep alive the traditional values of American democracy.

They are not really radical, these young idealists, no more radical, that is, than Jefferson's idea of freedom, Lincoln's idea of equality or Wilson's idea of a peaceful community of nations. Some of them, it is true, are taking what many regard as radical action, but they are doing it in defense of traditional values and in protest against the radical departure from those values embodied in the idea of an imperial destiny for America.

The focus of their protest is the war in Vietnam, and the measure of their integrity is the fortitude with which they refuse to be deceived about it. By striking contrast with the young Germans, who accepted the Nazi evil because the values of their society had disintegrated and they had no moral frame of reference, these young Americans are demonstrating the vitality of American values. They are demonstrating that, while their country is capable of acting falsely to itself, it cannot do so without internal disruption, without calling forth the regenerative counterforce of protest from Americans who are willing to act in defense of the principles they were brought up to believe in.

J. William Fulbright, *New York Times Magazine*, August 20, 1967, in William Dudley, ed., *The 1960s: Opposing Viewpoints*. San Diego: Greenhaven Press, 1997.

## Document 3: GIs United Against the War in Vietnam: Statement of Aims

*Opposition to the war was not limited to civilians. A small faction of active duty GIs also criticized U.S. involvement in Vietnam. The following selection is an excerpt of an antiwar statement made by GIs United Against the War in Vietnam, a group of army soldiers stationed in Vietnam.*

Fellow GIs:

For the past decade our country has been involved in a long, drawn-out, costly and tragic war in Vietnam. Most Americans do not support this war—increasing numbers are demonstrating their opposition, including active duty GIs. It is the most unpopular war in our history. Yet the government's policy threatens to continue this tragedy for many years to come.

Meanwhile, our country suffers while the slaughter goes on. The vast resources and sums of money the government squanders in support of a corrupt dictatorship in Saigon belong to the American people. It should be used to improve America, to make our country the shining example all of us want it to be—a free society—free of poverty and hunger, free of racial oppression, free of slums and illiteracy, and the misery they produce.

In addition, the rights and dignity of the black man in America have been trampled upon for the past 400 years. While being called upon to fight and die for so-called freedom, he has been forced to suffer racial oppression, discrimination, and social degradation within as well as outside the armed forces. Many black GIs are becoming increasingly aware of the hypocrisy of fighting against other people of color who are struggling for the same rights of self-determination as they are. Afro-Americans and all oppressed national minorities have the unconditional right to control their lives and determine their destinies as they see fit.

We, as GIs, are forced to suffer most of all in the Vietnam fiasco. Many of us were drafted into the Army against our will—nearly all of us are kept in its grasp against our will—all in order to carry out this illegal, immoral, and unjust war. We are forced to fight and die in a war we did not create and in which we don't believe.

This is not to mention the tens of thousands of innocent Vietnamese who are dying at our hands, many of them killed only because we can no longer tell the difference between them and our "enemies."

While all this goes on, the Army continues to trample on our rights as

well as our lives. All the crap, the harassment, dehumanization and contempt for the enlisted man that make "F.T.A." the three most popular letters in the Army goes on full swing in Nam, just like it does here.
Inspections, haircuts, saluting the brass, etc., are all part of the grind. And
there's a reason for it: the Army *has* to crush our spirit; it has to tamp the
humanity and individuality out of us so we won't be able to fight back.
This is an undemocratic war—the only way it can be fought is with an
undemocratic army, where GIs cannot be allowed to think, to discuss the
war and speak out against it, to influence and control policy.

But it is our right to be human. No one can take that from us—no one
has the right to rob us of our dignity, like the Army tries to do every day.
It is our right to think, and to speak out against an unjust war, to demonstrate our opposition if that is necessary. We are citizens of America even
if the Army would like to forget it, and these rights are guaranteed to us
by the Constitution of the United States.

The Army wants to take away our rights, to keep us from exercising
them so they can make us fight a war we don't want any part of. But the
Constitution says they can't do that. If we stand up for our rights and use
them the Army cannot stop us. If we speak out and demonstrate our opposition to the dirty war in Vietnam, no one can stop us. If we get together,
and if we get out and get the support of civilians, who are also against the
war, we can defend our rights and make our grievances known effectively.
If we can get together, we can win.

GIs United Against the War in Vietnam: Statement of Aims. The Sixties Project. http://lists.village.virginia.edu/
sixties/HTML_docs/Resources/Primary/Manifestos/GIs_United_aims.html.

## Document 4: Draft Resistance in the Vietnam Era

*Many Vietnam War dissenters demonstrated their opposition by resisting the
draft or encouraging others to do so. As a result, the number of conscientious objector exemptions reached unprecedented numbers. The statistics listed below, com-
piled by Paul W. Shaffer, do not include the thousands of men who resisted the
draft by illegal means.*

### Number of Draft Resisters

The Vietnam War era produced unprecedented numbers of war resisters.
If we examine the ratio of objector exemptions to actual inductions (per
100 inductions), we see very low numbers: World War I was 0.14 and
World War II was 0.15. However, in the Vietnam years, these numbers
went up, reaching 25 in 1970, and over 130 in 1972. This means that
toward the end of the Vietnam War, conscientious objector (CO) exemptions reached previously unthinkable proportions. In 1972, more young
men were exempted from the draft than were inducted into the armed services.

The following chart illustrates the growth of legal objections:

| Year/War | Ratio of Objector Exemptions to Actual Inductions (per 100 Inductions) |
|---|---|
| World War I | 0.14 |
| World War II | 0.15 |
| 1966 | 6.10 |
| 1967 | 8.11 |
| 1968 | 8.50 |
| 1969 | 13.45 |
| 1970 | 25.55 |
| 1971 | 42.62 |
| 1972 | 130.72 |
| 1973 | 73.30 |

Another indication of the rapid increase of COs during the Vietnam war was the fact that, in 1966, whereas about 200 COs were completing their two-year civilian service each month, twice that number were embarking on it. In addition to the many men who worked with the government to obtain the legal conscientious objector exemption, there were thousands of men who resisted the draft. Such refusal to cooperate with the Selective Service System was illegal, and it led to the indictment of over 20,000 men for draft law violations.

The human tidal wave of all these resisters and objectors, each one protesting the Vietnam war, was much larger than any anti-war movement in the United States for the other wars of the 20th century.

Paul W. Shaffer, "Draft Resistance in the Vietnam Era: Number of Draft Resisters." http://www.seas.upenn.edu/~pws/60s/numbers.html.

## Document 5: The Impudence of Student Demonstrators

*Student demonstrations—which expressed criticism of the Vietnam War, racial inequality, and American society in general often provoked anger from government officials. In a 1969 speech given at a Republican dinner, Spiro T. Agnew, vice president to Richard Nixon, assailed student demonstrators, calling them impudent and dangerous. Agnew served as vice president until 1973, when he left office after pleading no contest to charges of income tax evasion.*

A little over a week ago, I took a rather unusual step for a Vice President. I said something. Particularly, I said something that was predictably unpopular with the people who would like to run the country without the inconvenience of seeking public office. I said I did not like some of the things I saw happening in this country. I criticized those who encouraged government by street carnival and suggested it was time to stop the carousel.

It appears that by slaughtering a sacred cow I triggered a holy war. I have no regrets. I do not intend to repudiate my beliefs, recant my words, or run and hide.

What I said before, I will say again. It is time for the preponderant majority, the responsible citizens of this country, to assert *their* rights. It is time to stop dignifying the immature actions of arrogant, reckless, inexperienced elements within our society. The reason is compelling. It is simply that their tantrums are insidiously destroying the fabric of American democracy.

By accepting unbridled protest as a way of life, we have tacitly suggested that the great issues of our times are best decided by posturing and shouting matches in the streets. America today is drifting toward Plato's classic definition of a degenerating democracy—a democracy that permits the voice of the mob to dominate the affairs of government.

Last week I was lambasted for my lack of "mental and moral sensitivity." I say that any leader who does not perceive where persistent street struggles are going to lead this nation lacks mental acuity. And any leader who does not caution this nation on the danger of this direction lacks moral strength.

I believe in Constitutional dissent. I believe in the people registering their views with their elected representatives, and I commend those people who care enough about their country to involve themselves in its great issues. I believe in legal protest within the Constitutional limits of free speech, including peaceful assembly and the right of petition. But I do not believe that demonstrations, lawful or lawful, merit my approval or even my silence where the purpose is fundamentally unsound. In the case of the Vietnam Moratorium, the objects announced by the leaders—immediate unilateral withdrawal of all our forces from Vietnam—are not only unsound but idiotic . . . .

So great is the latitude of our liberty that only a subtle line divides use from abuse. I am convinced that our preoccupation with emotional demonstration, frequently crossing the line to civil disruption and even violence could inexorably lead us across that line forever.

## Evil Cloaked in Emotional Causes

Ironically, it is neither the greed nor the malicious but the self-righteous who are guilty of history's worse atrocities. Society understands greed and malice and erects barriers of law to defend itself from these vices. But evil cloaked in emotional causes is well disguised and often undiscovered until it is too late.

We have just such a group of self-proclaimed saviours of the American soul at work today. Relentless in their criticism of intolerance in America, they themselves are intolerant of those who differ with their views. In the name of academic freedom, they destroy academic freedom. Denouncing violence, they seize and vandalize buildings of great universities. Fiercely expressing their respect for truth, they disavow the logic and discipline necessary to pursue truth.

They would have us believe that they alone know what is good for America—what is true and right and beautiful. They would have us believe that their reflexive action is superior to our reflective action; that their revealed righteousness is more effective than our reason and experience. Think about it. Small bands of students are allowed to shut down great universities. Small groups of dissidents are allowed to shout down political candidates. Small cadres of professional protestors are allowed to jeopardize the peace efforts of the President of the United States.

It is time to question the credentials of their leaders. And, if in questioning we disturb a few people, I say it is time for them to be disturbed. If, in challenging, we polarize the American people, I say it is time for a positive polarization.

It is time for a healthy in-depth examination of policies and constructive realignment in this country. It is time to rip away the rhetoric and to divide on authentic lines. It is time to discard the fiction that in a country of 200 million people, everyone is qualified to quarterback the government . . . .

Now, we have among us a glib, activist element who would tell us our values are lies, and I call them impudent. Because anyone who impugns a legacy of liberty and dignity that reaches back to Moses, is impudent.

I call them snobs for most of them disdain to mingle with the masses who work for a living. They mock the common man's pride in his work, his family and his country. It has also been said that I called them intellectuals. I did not. I said that they characterized themselves as intellectuals. No true intellectual, no truly knowledgeable person, would so despise democratic institutions . . . .

Finally—and most important—regardless of the issue, it is time to stop demonstrating in the streets and start doing something constructive about our institutions. America must recognize the dangers of constant carnival. Americans must reckon with irresponsible leadership and reckless words. The mature and sensitive people of this country must realize that their freedom of protest is being exploited by avowed anarchists and communists who detest everything about this country and want to destroy it.

Spiro T. Agnew, "Impudence in the Streets," in Alexander Bloom and Wini Breines, eds., *"Takin' It to the Streets": A Sixties Reader*. New York: Oxford University Press, 1995.

## Document 6: The League for Spiritual Discovery

*While student demonstrators voiced their criticism of American society through rallies and marches, members of the youth counterculture expressed their discontent in other ways. Some hippies, frustrated with mainstream values, retreated into enclaves such as the League for Spiritual Discovery. Called LSD by its founder, Timothy Leary, the league attempted to gain spiritual enlightenment through the use of psychedelic drugs. The league's mission statement is excerpted below.*

1. The name of this organization to be incorporated in the state of New York

is the League for Spiritual Discovery—a non-profit religious association.

2. Purposes—The LSD has three general purposes—(a) individual worship, (b) communal worship and (c) public worship of God, based on revelation and empirically validated methods for spiritual discovery.

   (a) Individual Worship—Using Sacraments—To help each member to use the Sacraments to discover the divinity within and then express this revelation in an external life of harmony, beauty and particularly, to help each member to devote his complete consciousness and all his behavior to the glorification of God. Complete dedication to the life of worship is our aim, exemplified in the motto "Turn on, Tune-In, Drop-Out."

   (b) Communal Worship and Glorification—To maintain Ashrams (monastic centers) where renunciants (i.e. "drop outs"—those who take a vow to abandon secular activities for specified length of time) will live a communal life of worship and glorification. The community serves to facilitate individual illumination and to organize the liberation of energies to accomplish the evangelic and public mission of the League (see "c").

   (c) Public Illumination of the Human Race—To inform, teach, guide, liberate, illuminate other human beings, so that they can be initiated into a life of glorification and worship: the assumption here is that the modern civilization (as exemplified in American culture) is insane, destructive, warlike, materialistic, atheistic—a meaningless set of repetitious robot responses. The LSD aims to return man to a life of harmony with his own divinity—with his mate and family, with his fellow human beings, and with other natural energies—organic and inorganic—of this planet. A complete and rapid evolution of society is intended. Public celebrations will be held weekly in cities in this country and throughout the world.

3. Methods—The LSD is an orthodox, psychedelic religion. Like the founding group of every great world religion, the LSD aims to expand consciousness, to pursue internal union and revelation, and to express these revelations in actions of glorification.

   The SACRAMENTS of LSD are psychedelic chemicals which at every turning point in human history have been provided by God for man's illumination and liberation.

   The RITUALS of LSD are sensory, cellular and molecular psychedelic methods which have been discovered and passed on by religious masters of the past.

   (a) To go out of the mind and to come to the senses. Each League member devotes at least one hour a day to withdrawal from social, symbolic activity in order to attain sensory illumination, using the Sacraments marijuana or DMT. These methods include symbol

deprivation (meditation), solitude, silence, mantra (prayer), audi-
tory (psalm, religious music), postural, gestural, olfactory (incense),
tactile, gustatory, somatic (cakra exercises).

(b) Each League Member devotes at least one day a week away from
social-sensory-symbolic activities to attain communication with
evolutionary wisdom preserved in cellular and molecular structures. The Sacraments LSD, peyote, psilocybin are used for this
purpose.

Timothy Leary, League for Spiritual Discovery mission statement, 1967. http://leary.com/archives/text/
Archives/Millbrook/ChurchofLSD.html.


## Document 7: I Have a Dream

*Martin Luther King Jr. became involved in the struggle for racial equality in the
1950s when he organized a successful boycott of the segregated bus system in
Montgomery, Alabama. By the end of that decade, his inspirational speeches and
acts of nonviolent resistance had motivated a nationwide movement for civil
rights. King, recipient of the 1964 Nobel Peace Prize, led the campaign for civil
rights until his assassination in 1968. In his famous speech entitled "I Have a
Dream," delivered on August 28, 1963, in Washington, D.C., King expresses his
vision of racial harmony in America.*

Five score years ago, a great American, in whose symbolic shadow we
stand signed the Emancipation Proclamation. This momentous decree
came as a great beacon light of hope to millions of Negro slaves who had
been seared in the flames of withering injustice. It came as a joyous day-
break to end the long night of captivity.

But one hundred years later, we must face the tragic fact that the Negro
is still not free. One hundred years later, the life of the Negro is still sadly
crippled by the manacles of segregation and the chains of discrimination.
One hundred years later, the Negro lives on a lonely island of poverty in
the midst of a vast ocean of material prosperity. One hundred years later,
the Negro is still languishing in the corners of American society and finds
himself an exile in his own land. So we have come here today to dramatize
an appalling condition.

In a sense we have come to our nation's capital to cash a check. When
the architects of our republic wrote the magnificent words of the
Constitution and the Declaration of Independence, they were signing a
promissory note to which every American was to fall heir. This note was a
promise that all men would be guaranteed the inalienable rights of life, liberty, and the pursuit of happiness.

It is obvious today that America has defaulted on this promissory note
insofar as her citizens of color are concerned. Instead of honoring this
sacred obligation, America has given the Negro people a bad check which
has come back marked "insufficient funds." But we refuse to believe that

the bank of justice is bankrupt. We refuse to believe that there are insufficient funds in the great vaults of opportunity of this nation. So we have come to cash this check—a check that will give us upon demand the riches of freedom and the security of justice. We have also come to this hallowed spot to remind America of the fierce urgency of now. This is no time to engage in the luxury of cooling off or to take the tranquilizing drug of gradualism. Now is the time to rise from the dark and desolate valley of segregation to the sunlit path of racial justice. Now is the time to open the doors of opportunity to all of God's children. Now is the time to lift our nation from the quicksands of racial injustice to the solid rock of brotherhood.

It would be fatal for the nation to overlook the urgency of the moment and to underestimate the determination of the Negro. This sweltering summer of the Negro's legitimate discontent will not pass until there is an invigorating autumn of freedom and equality. Nineteen sixty-three is not an end, but a beginning. Those who hope that the Negro needed to blow off steam and will now be content will have a rude awakening if the nation returns to business as usual. There will be neither rest nor tranquility in America until the Negro is granted his citizenship rights. The whirlwinds of revolt will continue to shake the foundations of our nation until the bright day of justice emerges.

But there is something that I must say to my people who stand on the warm threshold which leads into the palace of justice. In the process of gaining our rightful place we must not be guilty of wrongful deeds. Let us not seek to satisfy our thirst for freedom by drinking from the cup of bitterness and hatred.

We must forever conduct our struggle on the high plane of dignity and discipline. We must not allow our creative protest to degenerate into physical violence. Again and again we must rise to the majestic heights of meeting physical force with soul force. The marvelous new militancy which has engulfed the Negro community must not lead us to distrust of all white people, for many of our white brothers, as evidenced by their presence here today, have come to realize that their destiny is tied up with our destiny and their freedom is inextricably bound to our freedom. We cannot walk alone.

And as we walk, we must make the pledge that we shall march ahead. We cannot turn back. There are those who are asking the devotees of civil rights, "When will you be satisfied?" We can never be satisfied as long as our bodies, heavy with the fatigue of travel, cannot gain lodging in the motels of the highways and the hotels of the cities. We cannot be satisfied as long as the Negro's basic mobility is from a smaller ghetto to a larger one. We can never be satisfied as long as a Negro in Mississippi cannot vote and a Negro in New York believes he has nothing for which to vote. No, no, we are not satisfied, and we will not be satisfied until justice rolls down like waters and righteousness like a mighty stream.

I am not unmindful that some of you have come here out of great trials and tribulations. Some of you have come fresh from narrow cells. Some of you have come from areas where your quest for freedom left you battered by the storms of persecution and staggered by the winds of police brutality. You have been the veterans of creative suffering. Continue to work with the faith that unearned suffering is redemptive.

Go back to Mississippi, go back to Alabama, go back to Georgia, go back to Louisiana, go back to the slums and ghettos of our northern cities, knowing that somehow this situation can and will be changed. Let us not wallow in the valley of despair.

I say to you today, my friends, that in spite of the difficulties and frustrations of the moment, I still have a dream. It is a dream deeply rooted in the American dream.

I have a dream that one day this nation will rise up and live out the true meaning of its creed: "We hold these truths to be self-evident: that all men are created equal."

I have a dream that one day on the red hills of Georgia the sons of former slaves and the sons of former slaveowners will be able to sit down together at a table of brotherhood.

I have a dream that one day even the state of Mississippi, a desert state, sweltering with the heat of injustice and oppression, will be transformed into an oasis of freedom and justice.

I have a dream that my four children will one day live in a nation where they will not be judged by the color of their skin but by the content of their character.

I have a dream today.

I have a dream that one day the state of Alabama, whose governor's lips are presently dripping with the words of interposition and nullification, will be transformed into a situation where little black boys and black girls will be able to join hands with little white boys and white girls and walk together as sisters and brothers.

I have a dream today.

I have a dream that one day every valley shall be exalted, every hill and mountain shall be made low, the rough places will be made plain, and the crooked places will be made straight, and the glory of the Lord shall be revealed, and all flesh shall see it together.

This is our hope. This is the faith with which I return to the South. With this faith we will be able to hew out of the mountain of despair a stone of hope. With this faith we will be able to transform the jangling discords of our nation into a beautiful symphony of brotherhood. With this faith we will be able to work together, to pray together, to struggle together, to go to jail together, to stand up for freedom together, knowing that we will be free one day.

This will be the day when all of God's children will be able to sing with a new meaning, "My country, 'tis of thee, sweet land of liberty, of thee I sing. Land where my fathers died, land of the pilgrim's pride, from every mountainside, let freedom ring."

And if America is to be a great nation this must become true. So let freedom ring from the prodigious hilltops of New Hampshire. Let freedom ring from the mighty mountains of New York. Let freedom ring from the heightening Alleghenies of Pennsylvania!

Let freedom ring from the snowcapped Rockies of Colorado!

Let freedom ring from the curvaceous peaks of California!

But not only that; let freedom ring from Stone Mountain of Georgia!

Let freedom ring from Lookout Mountain of Tennessee!

Let freedom ring from every hill and every molehill of Mississippi. From every mountainside, let freedom ring.

When we let freedom ring, when we let it ring from every village and every hamlet, from every state and every city, we will be able to speed up that day when all of God's children, black men and white men, Jews and Gentiles, Protestants and Catholics, will be able to join hands and sing in the words of the old Negro spiritual, "Free at last! free at last! thank God Almighty, we are free at last!"

Martin Luther King Jr., "I Have a Dream." Speech delivered in Washington, D.C., on August 28, 1963. http://web66.coled.umn.edu/new/MLK/MLK.html.

### Document 8: JFK's Radio and Television Report to the American People on Civil Rights

*John F. Kennedy, president from 1961 to 1963, was a vehement supporter of the civil rights movement. In the following selection, excerpted from a report delivered on June 11, 1963, Kennedy denounces the country's practice of racial segregation and discrimination. Less than six months later, Kennedy was assassinated in Dallas, Texas.*

This afternoon, following a series of threats and defiant statements, the presence of Alabama National Guardsmen was required on the University of Alabama to carry out the final and unequivocal order of the United States District Court of the Northern District of Alabama. That order called for the admission of two clearly qualified young Alabama residents who happened to have been born Negro.

That they were admitted peacefully on the campus is due in good measure to the conduct of the students of the University of Alabama, who met their responsibilities in a constructive way.

I hope that every American, regardless of where he lives, will stop and examine his conscience about this and other related incidents. This Nation was founded by men of many nations and backgrounds. It was founded on the principle that all men are created equal, and that the rights of every man are diminished when the rights of one man are threatened.

## Protecting the Rights of All Citizens

Today we are committed to a worldwide struggle to promote and protect the rights of all who wish to be free. And when Americans are sent to Vietnam or West Berlin, we do not ask for whites only. It ought to be possible, therefore, for American students of any color to attend any public institution they select without having to be backed up by troops.

It ought to be possible for American consumers of any color to receive equal service in places of public accommodation, such as hotels and restaurants and theaters and retail stores, without being forced to resort to demonstrations in the street, and it ought to be possible for American citizens of any color to register to vote in a free election without interference or fear of reprisal.

It ought to be possible, in short, for every American to enjoy the privileges of being American without regard to his race or his color. In short, every American ought to have the right to be treated as he would wish to be treated, as one would wish his children to be treated. But this is not the case.

The Negro baby born in America today, regardless of the section of the Nation in which he is born, has about one-half as much chance of completing a high school as a white baby born in the same place on the same day, one-third as much chance of completing college, one-third as much chance of becoming a professional man, twice as much chance of becoming unemployed, about one-seventh as much chance of earning $10,000 a year, a life expectancy which is 7 years shorter, and the prospects of earning only half as much.

This is not a sectional issue. Difficulties over segregation and discrimination exist in every city, in every State of the Union, producing in many cities a rising tide of discontent that threatens the public safety. Nor is this a partisan issue. In a time of domestic crisis men of good will and generosity should be able to unite regardless of party or politics. This is not even a legal or legislative issue alone. It is better to settle these matters in the courts than on the streets, and new laws are needed at every level, but law alone cannot make men see right.

We are confronted primarily with a moral issue. It is as old as the scriptures and is as clear as the American Constitution.

The heart of the question is whether all Americans are to be afforded equal rights and equal opportunities, whether we are going to treat our fellow Americans as we want to be treated. If an American, because his skin is dark, cannot eat lunch in a restaurant open to the public, if he cannot send his children to the best public school available, if he cannot vote for the public officials who will represent him, if, in short, he cannot enjoy the full and free life which all of us want, then who among us would be content to have the color of his skin changed and stand in his place? Who among us would then be content with the counsels of patience and delay?

One hundred years of delay have passed since President Lincoln freed the slaves, yet their heirs, their grandsons, are not fully free. They are not yet freed from the bonds of injustice. They are not yet freed from social and economic oppression. And this Nation, for all its hopes and all its boasts, will not be fully free until all its citizens are free.

We preach freedom around the world, and we mean it, and we cherish our freedom here at home, but are we to say to the world, and much more importantly, to each other that this is the land of the free except for the Negroes; that we have no second-class citizens except Negroes; that we have no class or caste system, no ghettoes, no master race except with respect to Negroes?

Now the time has come for this Nation to fulfill its promise. The events in Birmingham and elsewhere have so increased the cries for equality that no city or State or legislative body can prudently choose to ignore them.

The fires of frustration and discord are burning in every city, North and South, where legal remedies are not at hand. Redress is sought in the streets, in demonstrations, parades, and protests which create tensions and threaten violence and threaten lives.

## A Moral Crisis

We face, therefore, a moral crisis as a country and as a people. It cannot be met by repressive police action. It cannot be left to increased demonstrations in the streets. It cannot be quieted by token moves or talk. It is time to act in the Congress, in your State and local legislative body and, above all, in all of our daily lives.

It is not enough to pin the blame on others, to say this a problem of one section of the country or another, or deplore the fact that we face. A great change is at hand, and our task, our obligation, is to make that revolution, that change, peaceful and constructive for all.

Those who do nothing are inviting shame as well as violence. Those who act boldly are recognizing right as well as reality.

Next week I shall ask the Congress of the United States to act, to make a commitment it has not fully made in this century to the proposition that race has no place in American life or law. The Federal judiciary has upheld that proposition in the conduct of its affairs, including the employment of Federal personnel, the use of Federal facilities, and the sale of federally financed housing.

But there are other necessary measures which only the Congress can provide, and they must be provided at this session. The old code of equity law under which we live commands for every wrong a remedy, but in too many communities, in too many parts of the country, wrongs are inflicted on Negro citizens and there are no remedies at law. Unless the

Congress acts, their only remedy is in the street.

I am, therefore, asking the Congress to enact legislation giving all Americans the right to be served in facilities which are open to the public—hotels, restaurants, theaters, retail stores, and similar establishments.

This seems to me to be an elementary right. Its denial is an arbitrary indignity that no American in 1963 should have to endure, but many do.

## The Need for Voluntary Action

I have recently met with scores of business leaders urging them to take voluntary action to end this discrimination and I have been encouraged by their response, and in the last 2 weeks over 75 cities have seen progress made in desegregating these kinds of facilities. But many are unwilling to act alone, and for this reason, nationwide legislation is needed if we are to move this problem from the streets to the courts.

I am also asking the Congress to authorize the Federal Government to participate more fully in lawsuits designed to end segregation in public education. We have succeeded in persuading many districts to desegregate voluntarily. Dozens have admitted Negroes without violence. Today a Negro is attending a State-supported institution in every one of our 50 States, but the pace is very slow.

Too many Negro children entering segregated grade schools at the time of the Supreme Court's decision 9 years ago will enter segregated high schools this fall, having suffered a loss which can never be restored. The lack of an adequate education denies the Negro a chance to get a decent job.

The orderly implementation of the Supreme Court decision, therefore, cannot be left solely to those who may not have the economic resources to carry the legal action or who may be subject to harassment.

Other features will also be requested, including greater protection for the right to vote. But legislation, I repeat, cannot solve this problem alone. It must be solved in the homes of every American in every community across our country.

In this respect I want to pay tribute to those citizens North and South who have been working in their communities to make life better for all. They are acting not out of a sense of legal duty but out of a sense of human decency.

Like our soldiers and sailors in all parts of the world they are meeting freedom's challenge on the firing line, and I salute them for their honor and their courage.

My fellow Americans, this is a problem which faces us all—in every city of the North as well as the South. Today there are Negroes unemployed, two or three times as many compared to whites, inadequate in education, moving into the large cities, unable to find work, young people particularly out of work without hope, denied equal rights, denied the opportunity to eat at a restaurant or lunch counter or go to a movie theater, denied the right to a decent education, denied almost today the right to attend a State university even though qualified. It seems to me that these are matters which concern us all, not merely Presidents or Congressmen or Governors, but every citizen of the United States.

John F. Kennedy, *Radio and Television Report to the American People*. Report given at the White House on June 11, 1963. www.cs.umb.edu/jfklibrary/jo61163.htm.

## Document 9: An Interview with Malcolm X

*Malcolm X, an activist and leader of the Black Muslim church until his assassination in 1965, rejected Martin Luther King Jr.'s philosophy of nonviolence and called for blacks to achieve equality "by any means necessary." Malcolm X believed that the solution for racial problems in America was for blacks to revive a spirit of African nationalism. The following document is taken from an interview conducted by Présence Africaine, an African cultural organization located in Paris, on November 23, 1964.*

*Question*: How is it possible that some [civil rights leaders] are still preaching nonviolence?

*Malcolm X*: That's easy to understand—shows you the power of dollarism. The dollar makes anything possible. In nineteen-sixt— (I forget what year it was when the Sharpeville massacre took place in South Africa) if you read the testimony of [Nelson] Mandela in court, he brought up the fact that at that point the brothers in South Africa had begun to realize that they had to go into action, that nonviolence had become outdated: it only helped the enemy. But at the same time the enemy knows that once eleven million people stop being confined to a nonviolent approach against three million, you're going to have a different situation. They had to use their new modern tricks, so they ran down and got one of the Africans and gave him a glorious peace prize for being nonviolent, and it lent strength to the nonviolent image, to try and keep them a little nonviolent a little while longer. And it's the same way in the States. The black man in the States has begun to see that nonviolence is a trick that is put upon him to keep him from even being able to defend himself.

And so there's an increasing number of black people in America who are absolutely ready and willing to do whatever is necessary to see that their lives and their own property are protected by them.

So you have again your imperialists, and whatever else you call them, come along and give out another peace prize to again try and strengthen the image of nonviolence. This is their way of doing things, but everybody doesn't always accept those peace prizes . . . .

*Question:* Many black Americans are hoping you will be their leader. Do you have a determined political program and I would like to know, if you do have a political program which has already been set up, would you join this with a new organization which is called "Freedom Now"?

*Malcolm:* First, I don't profess to be anybody's leader. I'm one of 22 million Afro-Americans, all of whom have suffered the same things. And I probably cry out a little louder against the suffering than most others and therefore, perhaps, I'm better known.

I don't profess to have a political, economic, or social solution to a problem as complicated as the one which our people face in the States, but I am one of those who is willing to try *any means necessary* to bring an end to the injustices our people suffer.

One of the reasons why I say it's difficult to come up and say "this is the solution" or "that is the solution" is that a chicken cannot produce a duck egg, and it can't produce a duck egg because the system itself was produced by a chicken egg and can only reproduce what produced it.

The American system was produced from the enslavement of the black man. This political, economic, and social system of America was produced from the enslavement of the black man and that particular system is capable only of reproducing that out of which itself was produced. The only way a chicken can produce a duck egg [is] you have to revolutionize the system. . . .

*Question:* As a solution to this problem can one envisage the creation of an independent black state in the United States?

*Malcolm:* No! I wouldn't say "No, No." I wouldn't close the door to any solution. Our problem in the States is so deplorable we are justified to try anything—*anything.* Other independent states have been set up. They set up Israel and they weren't called separationists. But when we start talking about setting up something wherein we can rule ourselves, we're labeled separationists. But we are not separationists, nor are we integrationists. We're human beings.

*Question:* Brother Malcolm, can you foresee the day when the Negro race and culture will be respected in the world and even be predominant?

*Malcolm:* If I understand your question, brother, I have to say "Yes." I see the time when the black culture will be the dominant culture and when the black man will be the dominant man. And nobody should be against the black man being the dominant man. He's been dominated. I don't think that if we allow ourselves to be dominated it's wrong to pass the ball around once in a while. We've served everyone else, probably more so than anyone else has. We've permitted our continent to be raped and ravaged. We've permitted over 100 million human souls to be uprooted from the mother continent and shipped abroad, many of whom lost their lives at the bottom of the sea or were eaten by sharks. We've contributed to the economy of every country on the face of this earth with our slave labor. So if there's any kind of justice, if there's any kind of judgment, if there's any kind of God—then if he's coming to execute judgment or give some kind of justice—we have some bills that we haven't collected yet.

*Question:* Are you against the love between a black person and a white person?

*Malcolm:* How can anyone be against love? Whoever a person wants to love that's their business—that's like their religion . . . .

*Question:* Do you foresee a total assimilation with equal rights of the Afro-American into the white community of the United States in many, many years to come?

*Malcolm:* No! Nobody! Who's going to wait many years? I'm glad you asked the question like that because, you see, the oppressed never uses the same yardstick as the oppressor.

And this is what the oppressor doesn't realize. In his position of power he takes things for granted and he takes it for granted that everybody uses his yardstick. Well, today for a long time, we, the oppressed people, not only in America but in Africa, Asia and elsewhere, had to use someone else's yardstick. When they said "fast," what was "fast" to them was "fast" to us, but nowadays the yardstick has changed. We got our own yardstick. And when you say a long time this assimilation, or a long time this solution, the thing you don't realize is that other generations used a different yardstick. They had patience and you could tell them a long time and they would sit around a long time, but the young ones that's coming up now are asking "Why should he wait? Why should he have to wait for what other people have when they're born? Why should he have to go to a Supreme Court or to a Congress, or to a Senate, or to some kind of legislative body to be told he's a man when other people don't have to go through that process to be told that they're a man?" So you have a new generation coming up . . . . necessary to let the world know right now that they're going to be men or there just won't be a human being anywhere else.

*Question:* Is there a Negro movement in the United States that wishes to form a Negro state with the Africans?

*Malcolm:* Yes, they are important. There are an increasing number of Afro-Americans who want to migrate back to Africa. Now if it were to take place tomorrow you would probably have a limited number. So, in my opinion, if you wanted to solve the problem you would have to make the problem more digestible to a greater number of Afro-Americans. The idea is good but those who propagated the idea in the past put it to the public in the wrong way and because of this didn't get the desired result. The one who made the greatest impact was the honorable Marcus Garvey. And the United States government . . . put him in prison and charged him with fraud.

A spiritual "Back-to-Africa." If our people would try to migrate back to Africa culturally, first try to migrate back culturally and philosophically and psychologically, they would stay where they are physically but this psychological, cultural, philosophical migration would give us bonds with our mother continent that would strengthen our position in the country where we are right now, and then we'd be in a position to influence that government's policies and to keep them from supporting men like Tshombe.

*Question:* Brother Malcolm, don't you think there is a danger in the

United States that the Negroes will become diluted in the white majority?

*Malcolm:* Yes, brother, it does represent that danger but you can't ever have integration. They will never have integration in that country. Right now, if a Negro moves into a neighborhood, the white liberals are the first ones to move out. They can't integrate the schools in New York City. The United Nations diplomats are complaining that they're getting a beating for no other reason than their skin is dark—in New York City, not Mississippi. Integration would destroy our people, but we'll never have it in that country.

Malcolm X, *By Any Means Necessary*. New York: Pathfinder, 1992.

## Document 10: Black Panther Party Platform and Program

*The assassinations of advocates such as John F. Kennedy, Martin Luther King Jr., and Malcolm X inspired anger and frustration among African Americans and reinforced the belief that racial equality would never be achieved through traditional channels. In October 1966, the Black Panther Party demanded an immediate end to the oppression of blacks, claiming that if this demand was not met, the black community would establish its own government. The following document is a list of the Black Panther Party's tenets.*

1. *We want freedom. We want power to determine the destiny of our Black Community.*

   We believe that black people will not be free until we are able to determine our destiny.

2. *We want full employment for our people.*

   We believe that the federal government is responsible and obligated to give every man employment or a guaranteed income. We believe that if the white American businessmen will not give full employment, then the means of production should be taken from the businessmen and placed in the community so that the people of the community can organize and employ all of its people and give a high standard of living.

3. *We want an end to the robbery by the white man of our Black Community.*

   We believe that this racist government has robbed us and now we are demanding the overdue debt of forty acres and two mules. Forty acres and two mules was promised 100 years ago as restitution for slave labor and mass murder of black people. We will accept the payment as currency which will be distributed to our many communities. The Germans are now aiding the Jews in Israel for the genocide of the Jewish people. The Germans murdered six million Jews. The American racist has taken part in the slaughter of over twenty million black people; therefore, we feel that this is a modest demand that we make.

4. *We want decent housing, fit for shelter of human beings.*

   We believe that if the white landlords will not give decent housing to our black community, then the housing and the land should be made into cooperatives so that our community, with government aid, can build and make decent housing for its people.

5. *We want education for our people that exposes the true nature of this decadent American society. We want education that teaches us our true history and our role in the present-day society.*

We believe in an educational system that will give to our people a knowledge of self. If a man does not have knowledge of himself and his position in society and the world, then he has little chance to relate to anything else.

6. *We want all black men to be exempt from military service.*

We believe that Black people should not be forced to fight in the military service to defend a racist government that does not protect us. We will not fight and kill other people of color in the world who, like black people, are being victimized by the white racist government of America. We will protect ourselves from the force and violence of the racist police and the racist military, by whatever means necessary.

7. *We want an immediate end to police brutality and murder of black people.*

We believe we can end police brutality in our black community by organizing black self-defense groups that are dedicated to defending our black community from racist police oppression and brutality. The Second Amendment to the Constitution of the United States gives a right to bear arms. We therefore believe that all black people should arm themselves for self defense.

8. *We want freedom for all black men held in federal, state, county and city prisons and jails.*

We believe that all black people should be released from the many jails and prisons because they have not received a fair and impartial trial.

9. *We want all black people when brought to trial to be tried in court by a jury of their peer group or people from their black communities, as defined by the Constitution of the United States.*

We believe that the courts should follow the United States Constitution so that black people will receive fair trials. The 14th Amendment of the U.S. Constitution gives a man a right to be tried by his peer group. A peer is a person from a similar economic, social, religious, geographical, environmental, historical and racial background. To do this the court will be forced to select a jury from the black community from which the black defendant came. We have been, and are being tried by all-white juries that have no understanding of the "average reasoning man" of the black community.

10. *We want land, bread, housing, education, clothing, justice and peace. And as our major political objective, a United Nations–supervised plebiscite to be held throughout the black colony in which only black colonial subjects will be allowed to participate for the purpose of determining the will of black people as to their national destiny.*

When in the course of human events, it becomes necessary for one people to dissolve the political bands which have connected them with another, and to assume, among the powers of the earth, the separate and equal station to which the laws of nature and nature's God entitle them, a decent respect to the opinions of mankind requires that they should declare the causes which impel them to the separation.

We hold these truths to be self evident, that all men are created equal; that they are endowed by their Creator with certain unalienable rights; that among these are life, liberty, and the pursuit of happiness. *That, to secure these rights, governments are instituted among men, deriving their just powers from the consent of the governed; that, whenever any form of government becomes destructive of these ends, it is the right of the people to alter or to abolish it, and to institute a new government, laying its foundation on such principles, and organizing its powers in such form, as to them shall seem most likely to effect their safety and happiness.* Prudence, indeed, will dictate that governments long established should not be changed for light and transient causes; and accordingly, all experience hath shown, that mankind are more disposed to suffer, while evils are sufferable, than to right themselves by abolishing the forms to which they are accustomed. *But, when a long train of abuses and usurpations, pursuing invariable the same object, evinces a design to reduce them under absolute despotism, it is their right, it is their duty, to throw off such government, and to provide new guards for their future security.*

*October 1966 Black Panther Party Platform and Program.* The Sixties Project. http://lists.village.virginia.edu/sixties/ HTML_docs/Resources/Primary/Manifestos/Panther_platform.html.

## Document 11: The Problem That Has No Name

*In the late 1950s, Betty Friedan, a mother and scholar living in New York, began to document the discontent she witnessed among American housewives—a discontent that she labeled "the problem that has no name." In 1963, Friedan published the results of her study in* The Feminine Mystique, *a book that is considered by some to be the catalyst of the feminist movement. In the excerpt below, Friedan describes how women of the late fifties and early sixties felt stifled by traditional gender roles.*

In 1960, the problem that has no name burst like a boil through the image of the happy American housewife. In the television commercials the pretty housewives still beamed over their foaming dishpans and Time's cover story on "The Suburban Wife, an American Phenomenon" protested: "Having too good a time . . . to believe that they should be unhappy." But the actual unhappiness of the American housewife was suddenly being reported, from the *New York Times* and *Newsweek* to *Good Housekeeping* and

CBS Television ("The Trapped Housewife"), although almost everybody who talked about it found some superficial reason to dismiss it. It was attributed to incompetent appliance repairmen (*New York Times*), or the distances children must be chauffeured in the suburbs (*Time*), or too much PTA (*Redbook*). Some said it was the old problem—education: more and more women had education, which naturally made them unhappy in their role as housewives. "The road from Freud to Frigidaire; from Sophocles to Spock, has turned out to be a bumpy one," reported the New York Times (June 28, 1960). "Many young women—certainly not all—whose education plunged them into a world of ideas feel stifled in their homes. They find their routine lives out of joint with their training. Like shut-ins, they feel left out. In the last year, the problem of the educated housewife has provided the meat of dozens of speeches made by troubled presidents of women's colleges who maintain, in the face of complaints, that sixteen years of academic training is realistic preparation for wifehood and motherhood."

There was much sympathy for the educated housewife. ("Like a two-headed schizophrenic . . . once she wrote a paper on the Graveyard poets; now she writes notes to the milkman. Once she determined the boiling point of sulphuric acid; now she determines her boiling point with the overdue repairman. The housewife often is reduced to screams and tears. . . . No one, it seems, is appreciative, least of all herself, of the kind of person she becomes in the process of turning from poetess into shrew.")

Home economists suggested more realistic preparation for housewives, such as high-school workshops in home appliances. College educators suggested more discussion groups on home management and the family, to prepare women for the adjustment to domestic life. A spate of articles appeared in the mass magazines offering "Fifty-eight Ways to Make Your Marriage More Exciting." No month went by without a new book by a psychiatrist or sexologist offering technical advice on finding greater fulfillment through sex.

A male humorist joked in *Harper's Bazaar* (July, 1960) that the problem could be solved by taking away woman's right to vote. ("In the pre-19th Amendment era, the American woman was placid, sheltered and sure of her role in American society. She left all the political decisions to her husband and he, in turn, left all the family decisions to her. Today a woman has to make both the family and the political decisions, and it's too much for her.")

A number of educators suggested seriously that women no longer be admitted to the four-year colleges and universities: in the growing college crisis, the education which girls could not use as housewives was more urgently needed than ever by boys to do the work of the atomic age.

The problem was also dismissed with drastic solutions no one could take seriously. (A woman writer proposed in *Harper's* that women be drafted for compulsory service as nurses' aides and baby-sitters.) And it was smoothed over with the age-old panaceas: "love is their answer," "the only answer is inner help," "the secret of completeness—children,'" a private means of intellectual fulfillment," "to cure this toothache of the spir-it—the simple formula of handing one's self and one's will over to God."

The problem was dismissed by telling the housewife she doesn't realize how lucky she is—her own boss, no time clock, no junior executive gun-ning for your job. What if she isn't happy?—does she think men are happy in this world? Does she really, secretly, still want to be a man? Doesn't she know yet how lucky she is to be a woman?

### No Solutions

The problem was also, and finally, dismissed by shrugging that there are no solutions: this is what being a woman means, and what is wrong with American women that they can't accept their role gracefully? As *Newsweek* put it (March 7, 1960):

> She is dissatisfied with a lot that women of other lands can only dream of. Her discontent is deep, pervasive, and impervious to the superficial remedies which are offered at every hand. . . . An army of professional explorers have already charted the major sources of trouble. . . . From the beginning of time, the female cycle has defined and confined woman's role. As Freud was credited with saying: "Anatomy is destiny." Though no group of women has ever pushed these natural restrictions as far as the American wife, it seems that she still cannot accept them with good grace. . . . A young mother with a beautiful family, charm, talent and brains is apt to dismiss her role apologeti-cally. "What do I do?" you hear her say. "Why nothing. I'm just a housewife." A good education, it seems, has given this paragon among women an understanding of the value of every-thing except her own worth. . . .

And so she must accept the fact that "American women's unhappiness is merely the most recently won of women's rights," and adjust and say with the happy housewife found by *Newsweek:* "We ought to salute the won-derful freedom we all have and be proud of our lives today. I have had col-lege and I've worked, but being a housewife is the most rewarding and sat-isfying role. . . . My mother was never included in my father's business affairs . . . she couldn't get out of the house and away from us children. But I am an equal to my husband; I can go along with him on business trips and to social business affairs."

The alternative offered was a choice that few women would contem-plate. In the sympathetic words of the *New York Times:* "All admit to being deeply frustrated at times by the lack of privacy, the physical burden, the routine of family life, the confinement of it. However, none would give up her home and family if she had the choice to make again." *Redbook* com-mented: "Few women would want to thumb their noses at husbands, chil-dren and community and go off on their own. Those who do may be tal-ented individuals, but they rarely are successful women."

### Growing Discontent

The year American women's discontent boiled over, it was also reported (*Look*) that the more than 21,000,000 American women who are single, widowed, or divorced do not cease even after fifty their frenzied, desperate search for a man. And the search begins early—for seventy percent of all American women now marry before they are twenty-four. A pretty twenty-five-year-old secretary took thirty-five different jobs in six months in the futile hope of finding a husband. Women were moving from one political club to another, taking evening courses in accounting or sailing, learning to play golf or ski, joining a number of churches in succession, going to bars alone, in their ceaseless search for a man.

Of the growing thousands of women currently getting private psychiatric help in the United States, the married ones were reported dissatisfied with their marriages, the unmarried ones suffering from anxiety and, finally, depression. Strangely, a number of psychiatrists stated that, in their experience, unmarried women patients were happier than married ones. So the door of all those pretty suburban houses opened a crack to permit a glimpse of uncounted thousands of American housewives who suffered alone from a problem that suddenly everyone was talking about, and beginning to take for granted, as one of those unreal problems in American life that can never be solved—like the hydrogen bomb. By 1962 the plight of the trapped American housewife had become a national parlor game. Whole issues of magazines, newspaper columns, books learned and frivolous, educational conferences and television panels were devoted to the problem.

Even so, most men, and some women, still did not know that this problem was real. But those who had faced it honestly knew that all the superficial remedies, the sympathetic advice, the scolding words and the cheering words were somehow drowning the problem in unreality. A bitter laugh was beginning to be heard from American women. They were admired, envied, pitied, theorized over until they were sick of it, offered drastic solutions or silly choices that no one could take seriously. They got all kinds of advice from the growing armies of marriage and child guidance counselors, psychotherapists, and armchair psychologists, on how to adjust to their role as housewives. No other road to fulfillment was offered to American women in the middle of the twentieth century. Most adjusted to their role and suffered or ignored the problem that has no name. It can be less painful, for a woman, not to hear the strange, dissatisfied voice stirring within her.

Betty Friedan, *The Feminine Mystique*. New York: W. W. Norton, 1963.

### Document 12: The National Organization for Women Statement of Purpose

*October 29, 1966, marked the official beginning of the National Organization for Women (NOW), a group of women working for the abolition of prejudice and discrimination against women. On this date, Betty Friedan, author of* The Feminine Mystique *and NOW's founder and president, announced the organization's goals at a conference in Washington, D.C.*

We, men and women, who hereby constitute ourselves as the National Organization for Women, believe that the time has come for a new movement toward true equality for all women in America, and toward a fully equal partnership of the sexes, as part of the world-wide revolution of human rights now taking place within and beyond our national borders.

The purpose of NOW is to take action to bring women into full participation in the mainstream of American society now, exercising all the privileges and responsibilities thereof in truly equal partnership with men.

We believe the time has come to move beyond the abstract argument, discussion and symposia over the status and special nature of women which has raged in America in recent years; the time has come to confront, with concrete action, the conditions that now prevent women from enjoying the equality of opportunity and freedom of which is their right, as individual Americans, and as human beings.

NOW is dedicated to the proposition that women, first and foremost, are human beings, who, like all other people in our society, must have the chance to develop their fullest human potential. We believe that women can achieve such equality only by accepting to the full the challenges and responsibilities they share with all other people in our society, as part of the decision-making mainstream of American political, economic and social life.

We organize to initiate or support action, nationally, or in any part of this nation, by individuals or organizations, to break through the silken curtain of prejudice and discrimination against women in government, industry, the professions, the churches, the political parties, the judiciary, the labor unions, in education, science, medicine, law, religion and every other field of importance in American society. Enormous changes taking place in our society make it both possible and urgently necessary to advance the unfinished revolution of women toward true equality, now. With a life span lengthened to nearly 75 years it is no longer either necessary or possible for women to devote the greater part of their lives to child-rearing; yet childbearing and rearing—which continues to be a most important part of most women's lives—still is used to justify barring women from equal professional and economic participation and advance.

Today's technology has reduced most of the productive chores which women once performed in the home and in mass-production industries based upon routine unskilled labor. This same technology has virtually eliminated the quality of muscular strength as a criterion for filling most jobs, while intensifying American industry's need for creative intelligence. In view of this new industrial revolution created by automation in the mid–twentieth century, women can and must participate in old and new fields of society in full equality—or become permanent outsiders.

## The Declining Position of Women

Despite all the talk about the status of American women in recent years, the actual position of women in the United States has declined, and is declining, to an alarming degree throughout the 1950's and '60s. Although 46.4% of all American women between the ages of 18 and 65 now work outside the home, the overwhelming majority—75%—are in routine clerical, sales, or factory jobs, or they are household workers, cleaning women, hospital attendants.

About two-thirds of Negro women workers are in the lowest paid service occupations. Working women are becoming increasingly—not less—concentrated on the bottom of the job ladder. As a consequence full-time women workers today earn on the average only 60% of what men earn, and that wage gap has been increasing over the past twenty-five years in every major industry group. In 1964, of all women with a yearly income, 89% earned under $5,000 a year; half of all full-time year round women workers earned less than $3,690; only 1.4% of full-time year round women workers had an annual income of $10,000 or more.

Further, with higher education increasingly essential in today's society, too few women are entering and finishing college or going on to graduate or professional school. Today, women earn only one in three of the B.A.'s and M.A.'s granted, and one in ten of the Ph.D.'s.

In all the professions considered of importance to society, and in the executive ranks of industry and government, women are losing ground. Where they are present it is only a token handful. Women comprise less than 1% of federal judges; less than 4% of all lawyers; 7% of doctors. Yet women represent 51% of the U.S. population. And, increasingly men are replacing women in the top positions in secondary and elementary schools, in social work, and in libraries—once thought to be women's fields.

Official pronouncements of the advance in the status of women hide not only the reality of this dangerous decline, but the fact that nothing is being done to stop it. The excellent reports of the President's Commission on the Status of Women and of the State Commissions have not been fully implemented. Such Commissions have power only to advise. They have no power to enforce their recommendations; nor have they the freedom to organize American women and men to press for action on them. The reports of these commissions have, however, created a basis upon which it is now possible to build.

Discrimination in employment on the basis of sex is now prohibited by federal law, in Title VII of the Civil Rights Act of 1964. But although nearly one-third of the cases brought before the Equal Employment Opportunity Commission during the first year dealt with sex discrimination and the proportion is increasing dramatically, the Commission has not made clear its intention to enforce the law with the same seriousness on behalf of women as of other victims of discrimination. Many of these cases were Negro women, who are the victims of the double discrimination of race and sex. Until now, too few women's organizations and official spokesmen have been willing to speak out against these dangers facing women. Too many women have been restrained by the fear of being called "feminist."

## NOW's Major Tenets

There is no civil rights movement to speak for women, as there has been for Negroes and other victims of discrimination. The National Organization for Women must therefore begin to speak.

WE BELIEVE that the power of American law, and the protection guaranteed by the U.S. Constitution to the civil rights of all individuals, must be effectively applied and enforced to isolate and remove patterns of sex discrimination, to ensure equality of opportunity in employment and education, and equality of civil and political rights and responsibilities on behalf of women, as well as for Negroes and other deprived groups.

We realize that women's problems are linked to many broader questions of social justice; their solution will require concerted action by many groups. Therefore, convinced that human rights for all are indivisible, we expect to give active support to the common cause of equal rights for all those who suffer discrimination and deprivation, and we call upon other organizations committed to such goals to support our efforts toward equality for women.

WE DO NOT ACCEPT the token appointment of a few women to high-level positions in government and industry as a substitute for a serious continuing effort to recruit and advance women according to their individual abilities. To this end, we urge American government and industry to mobilize the same resources of ingenuity and command with which they have solved problems of far greater difficulty than those now impeding the progress of women.

WE BELIEVE that this nation has a capacity at least as great as other nations, to innovate new social institutions which will enable women to enjoy true equality of opportunity and responsibility in society, without conflict with their responsibilities as mothers and homemakers. In such innovations, America does not lead the Western world, but lags by decades behind many European countries. We do not accept the traditional assumption that a woman has to choose between marriage and motherhood, on the one hand, and serious participation in industry or the professions on the other. We question the present expectation that all normal women will retire from job or profession for 10 or 15 years, to devote their full time to raising children, only to reenter the job market at a relatively minor level. This in itself, is a deterrent to the aspirations of women, to their acceptance into management or professional training courses, and to the very possibility of equality of opportunity or real choice, for all but a few women. Above all, we reject the assumption that these problems are the unique responsibility of each individual woman, rather than a basic social dilemma which society must solve. True equality of opportunity and free-dom of choice for women requires such practical, and possible innovations as a nationwide network of child-care centers which will make it unneces-sary for women to retire completely from society until their children are grown, and national programs to provide retraining for women who have chosen to care for their own children full-time.

WE BELIEVE that it is as essential for every girl to be educated to her full potential of human ability as it is for every boy—with the knowledge that such education is the key to effective participation in today's economy and that, for a girl as for a boy, education can only be serious where there is expectation that it be used in society. We believe that American educa-tors are capable of devising means of imparting such expectations to girl students. Moreover, we consider the decline in the proportion of women receiving higher and professional education to be evidence of discrimina-tion. This discrimination may take the form of quotas against the admission of women to colleges, and professional schools; lack of encouragement by parents, counselors and educators; denial of loans or fellowships; or the tra-ditional or arbitrary procedures in graduate and professional training geared in terms of men, which inadvertently discriminate against women. We believe that the same serious attention must be given to high school dropouts who are girls as to boys.

WE REJECT the current assumptions that a man must carry the sole burden of supporting himself, his wife, and family, and that a woman is automatically entitled to lifelong support by a man upon her marriage, or that marriage, home and family are primarily woman's world and responsi-bility—hers to dominate—his to support. We believe that a true partner-ship between the sexes demands a different concept of marriage, an equi-table sharing of the responsibilities of home and children and of the eco-nomic burdens of their support. We believe that proper recognition should be given to the economic and social value of homemaking and child-care. To these ends we will seek to open a reexamination of laws and mores gov-erning marriage and divorce, for we believe that the current state of "half-equality" between the sexes discriminates against both men and women, and is the cause of much unnecessary hostility between the sexes.

WE BELIEVE that women must now exercise their political rights and responsibility as American citizens. They must refuse to be segregated on the basis of sex into separate-and-not-equal ladies auxiliaries in the politi-cal parties, and they must demand representation according to their num-bers in the regularly constituted party committees—at local, state, and national levels—and in the informal power structure, participating fully in the selection of candidates and political decision-making, and running for office themselves.

IN THE INTERESTS OF THE HUMAN DIGNITY OF WOMEN, we will protest, and endeavor to change, the false image of women now prevalent in the mass media, and in the texts, ceremonies, laws, and practices of our major social institutions. Such images perpetuate contempt for women by society and by women for themselves. We are similarly opposed to all policies and practices—in church, state, college, factory, or office—which, in the guise of protectiveness, not only deny opportunities but also foster in women self-denigration, dependence, and evasion of responsibility, undermine their confidence in their own abilities and foster contempt for women.

NOW WILL HOLD ITSELF INDEPENDENT OF ANY POLITICAL PARTY in order to mobilize the political power of all women and men intent on our goals. We will strive to ensure that no party, candidate, president, senator, governor, congressman, or any public official who betrays or ignores the principle of full equality between the sexes is elected or appointed to office. If it is necessary to mobilize the votes of men and women who believe in our cause, in order to win for women the final right to be fully free and equal human beings, we so commit ourselves.

WE BELIEVE THAT women will do most to create a new image of women by acting now, and by speaking out in behalf of their own equality, freedom, and human dignity—not in pleas for special privilege, nor in enmity toward men, who are also victims of the current, half-equality between the sexes—but in an active, self-respecting partnership with men. By so doing, women will develop confidence in their own ability to determine actively, in partnership with men, the conditions of their life, their choices, their future and their society.

*National Organization for Women Statement of Purpose*, 1966. http://history.hanover.edu/courses/excerpts/111now.html.

## Document 13: The Redstockings Manifesto

*Radical feminists of the late 1960s felt that the women's liberation movement was wrong to blame sexism on institutions or social roles. New feminist groups, such as the Redstockings collective, identified men as the agents of women's oppression. The 1969 Redstockings Manifesto, excerpted below, contends that men have used their power to keep women in an inferior position.*

I. After centuries of individual and preliminary political struggle, women are uniting to achieve their final liberation from male supremacy. Redstockings is dedicated to building this unity and winning our freedom.

II. Women are an oppressed class. Our oppression is total, affecting every facet of our lives. We are exploited as sex objects, breeders, domestic servants, and cheap labor. We are considered inferior beings, whose only purpose is to enhance men's lives. Our humanity is denied. Our prescribed behavior is enforced by the threat of physical violence.

Because we have lived so intimately with our oppressors, in isolation from each other, we have been kept from seeing our personal suffering as a political condition. This creates the illusion that a woman's relationship with her man is a matter of interplay between two unique personalities, and can be worked out individually. In reality, every such relationship is a *class* relationship, and the conflicts between individual men and women are *political* conflicts that can only be solved collectively.

III. We identify the agents of our oppression as men. Male supremacy is the oldest, most basic form of domination. All other forms of exploitation and oppression (racism, capitalism, imperialism, etc.) are extensions of male supremacy; men dominate women, a few men dominate the rest. All power structures throughout history have been male-dominated and male-oriented. Men have controlled all political, economic, and cultural institutions and backed up this control with physical force. They have used their power to keep women in an inferior position. *All men* receive economic, sexual, and psychological benefits from male supremacy. *All men* have oppressed women.

IV. Attempts have been made to shift the burden of responsibility from men to institutions or to women themselves. We condemn these arguments as evasions. Institutions alone do not oppress; they are merely tools of the oppressor. To blame institutions implies that men and women are equally victimized, obscures the fact that men benefit from the subordination of women, and gives men the excuse that they are forced to be oppressors. On the contrary, any man is free to renounce his superior position provided that he is willing to be treated like a woman by other men.

We also reject the idea that women consent to or are to blame for their own oppression. Women's submission is not the result of brainwashing, stupidity, or mental illness but of continual, daily pressure from men. We do not need to change ourselves, but to change men.

The most slanderous evasion of all is that women can oppress men. The basis for this illusion is the isolation of individual relationships from their political context and the tendency of men to see any legitimate challenge to their privileges as persecution.

V. We regard our personal experience, and our feelings about that experience, as the basis for an analysis of our common situation. We cannot rely on existing ideologies as they are all products of male supremacist culture. We question every generalization and accept none that are not confirmed by our experience.

Our chief task at present is to develop female class consciousness through sharing experience and publicly exposing the sexist foundation of all our institutions. Consciousness-raising is not "therapy," which implies the existence of individual solutions and falsely assumes that the male-female relationship is purely personal, but the only method by which we can ensure that our program for liberation is based on the concrete realities of our lives.

The first requirement for raising class consciousness is honesty, in private and in public, with ourselves and other women.

VI. We identify with all women. We define our best interest as that of the poorest, most brutally exploited woman.

We repudiate all economic, racial, educational, or status privileges that divide us from other women. We are determined to recognize and eliminate any prejudices we may hold against other women.

We are committed to achieving internal democracy. We will do whatever is necessary to ensure that every woman in our movement has an equal chance to participate, assume responsibility, and develop her political potential.

VII. We call on all our sisters to unite with us in struggle.We call on all men to give up their male privileges and support women's liberation in the interest of our humanity and their own.

In fighting for our liberation, we will always take the side of women against their oppressors. We will not ask what is "revolutionary" or "reformist," only what is good for women.

The time for individual skirmishes has passed. This time we are going all the way.

Shulamith Firestone and Ellen Willis, "Redstockings Manifesto," in Miriam Schneir, ed., *Feminism in Our Time: The Essential Writings, World War II to the Present*. New York: Vintage Books, 1994.

## Document 14: The Great Society

*One of the most lasting legislative developments of the 1960s was President Lyndon B. Johnson's Great Society legislation, which increased government's role in ameliorating social problems. This legislation provided federal aid for education, urban renewal, and housing; developed a War on Poverty program; and established Medicare and Medicaid. Today, Great Society legislation is the source of political controversy between Democrats, who favor federal funding of social programs, and Republicans, who wish to limit the role of government.*

The purpose of protecting the life of our Nation and preserving the liberty of our citizens is to pursue the happiness of our people. Our success in that pursuit is the test of our success as a Nation.

For a century we labored to settle and to subdue a continent. For half a century we called upon unbounded invention and untiring industry to create an order of plenty for all of our people.

The challenge of the next half century is whether we have the wisdom to use that wealth to enrich and elevate our national life, and to advance the quality of our American civilization.

Your imagination, your initiative, and your indignation will determine whether we build a society where progress is the servant of our needs, or a society where old values and new visions are buried under unbridled growth. For in your time we have the opportunity to move not only toward the rich society and the powerful society, but upward to the Great Society.

### Creating a Great Society

The Great Society rests on abundance and liberty for all. It demands an end to poverty and racial injustice, to which we are totally committed in our time. But that is just the beginning.

The Great Society is a place where every child can find knowledge to enrich his mind and to enlarge his talents. It is a place where leisure is a welcome chance to build and reflect, not a feared cause of boredom and restlessness. It is a place where the city of man serves not only the needs of the body and the demands of commerce but the desire for beauty and the hunger for community.

It is a place where man can renew contact with nature. It is a place which honors creation for its own sake and for what it adds to the understanding of the race. It is a place where men are more concerned with the quality of their goals than the quantity of their goods.

But most of all, the Great Society is not a safe harbor, a resting place, a final objective, a finished work. It is a challenge constantly renewed, beckoning us toward a destiny where the meaning of our lives matches the marvelous products of our labor.

So I want to talk to you today about three places where we begin to build the Great Society—in our cities, in our countryside, and in our classrooms.

Many of you will live to see the day, perhaps 50 years from now, when there will be 400 million Americans—four-fifths of them in urban areas. In the remainder of this century urban population will double, city land will double, and we will have to build homes, highways, and facilities equal to all those built since this country was first settled. So in the next 40 years we must re-build the entire urban United States.

## The State of American Cities

Aristotle said: "Men come together in cities in order to live, but they remain together in order to live the good life." It is harder and harder to live the good life in American cities today.

The catalog of ills is long: there is the decay of the centers and the despoiling of the suburbs. There is not enough housing for our people or transportation for our traffic. Open land is vanishing and old landmarks are violated.

Worst of all, expansion is eroding the precious and time honored values of community with neighbors and communion with nature. The loss of these values breeds loneliness and boredom and indifference.

Our society will never be great until our cities are great. Today the frontier of imagination and innovation is inside those cities and not beyond their borders.

New experiments are already going on. It will be the task of your generation to make the American city a place where future generations will come, not only to live but to live the good life.

I understand that if I stayed here tonight I would see that Michigan students are really doing their best to live the good life.

This is the place where the Peace Corps was started. It is inspiring to see how all of you, while you are in this country, are trying so hard to live at the level of the people.

## Protecting America's Countryside

A second place where we begin to build the Great Society is in our countryside. We have always prided ourselves on being not only America the strong and America the free, but America the beautiful. Today that beauty is in danger. The water we drink, the food we eat, the very air that we breathe, are threatened with pollution. Our parks are overcrowded, our seashores overburdened. Green fields and dense forests are disappearing.

A few years ago we were greatly concerned about the "Ugly American." Today we must act to prevent an ugly America.

For once the battle is lost, once our natural splendor is destroyed, it can never be recaptured. And once man can no longer walk with beauty or wonder at nature his spirit will wither and his sustenance be wasted.

## Expanding Educational Opportunities

A third place to build the "Great Society" is in the classrooms of America. There your children's lives will be shaped. Our society will not be great until every young mind is set free to scan the farthest reaches of thought and imagination. We are still far from that goal.

Today, 8 million adult Americans, more than the entire population of Michigan, have not finished 5 years of school. Nearly 20 million have not finished 8 years of school. Nearly 54 million—more than one quarter of all America—have not even finished high school.

Each year more than 100,000 high school graduates, with proved ability, do not enter college because they cannot afford it. And if we cannot educate today's youth, what will we do in 1970 when elementary school enrollment will be 5 million greater than 1960? And high school enrollment will rise by 5 million. College enrollment will increase by more than 3 million.

In many places, classrooms are overcrowded and curricula are outdated. Most of our qualified teachers are underpaid, and many of our paid teachers are unqualified. So we must give every child a place to sit and a teacher to learn from. Poverty must not be a bar to learning, and learning must offer an escape from poverty.

But more classrooms and more teachers are not enough. We must seek an educational system which grows in excellence as it grows in size. This means better training for our teachers. It means preparing youth to enjoy their hours of leisure as well as their hours of labor. It means exploring new techniques of teaching, to find new ways to stimulate the love of learning and the capacity for creation.

These are three of the central issues of the Great Society. While our Government has many programs directed at those issues, I do not pretend that we have the full answer to those problems.

But I do promise this: We are going to assemble the best thought and the broadest knowledge from all over the world to find those answers for

America. I intend to establish working groups to prepare a series of White House conferences and meetings—on the cities, on natural beauty, on the quality of education, and on other emerging challenges. And from these meetings and from this inspiration and from these studies we will begin to set our course toward the Great Society.

The solution to these problems does not rest on a massive program in Washington, nor can it rely solely on the strained resources of local authority. They require us to create new concepts of cooperation, a creative federalism, between the National Capital and the leaders of local communities.

Lyndon B. Johnson, "Great Society Speech," 1964. http://hs1.hst.msu.edu/~hst306/documents/great.html.

# CHRONOLOGY

**February 1, 1960**
Four black college students stage a sit-in protest against racial discrimination at a Woolworth's lunch counter in Greensboro, North Carolina.

**April 1960**
The Student Nonviolent Coordinating Committee (SNCC) is founded to coordinate the growing civil rights sit-in movement.

**May 1, 1960**
U-2 spy plane pilot Francis Gary Powers is shot down over the Soviet Union; the incident worsens U.S.-Soviet relations.

**May 9, 1960**
The federal government approves the first birth-control pill as safe for general use.

**September 26, 1960**
Candidates Richard M. Nixon and John F. Kennedy engage in the nation's first televised presidential campaign debate.

**November 8, 1960**
Kennedy defeats Nixon in the closest presidential election since 1888.

**January 3, 1961**
The United States breaks off diplomatic relations with Cuba.

**March 1, 1961**
President Kennedy establishes the Peace Corps.

**March 21, 1961**
The United States sends military advisers and aid to Laos.

**April 17, 1961**
The Bay of Pigs fiasco: American-trained and -supplied Cuban exiles fail in their efforts to depose Fidel Castro.

**May 5, 1961**
Alan Shepard becomes the first American in space.

**May 25, 1961**
President Kennedy pledges to put an American on the moon by the end of the decade.

**August 13, 1961**
East Germany closes the Berlin border and begins construction of the Berlin Wall.

## December 11, 1961
Kennedy sends four hundred American combat troops to South Vietnam.

## 1962
In *Engel v. Vitale* the Supreme Court rules that even a nondenominational prayer in a public school is unconstitutional; in *Baker v. Carr* it is ruled that legislative districts must be relatively equal in population.

Michael Harrington publishes *The Other America*, detailing the problem of poverty in the United States; *Silent Spring* by Rachel Carson raises public consciousness of environmental degradation.

## February 20, 1962
John Glenn becomes the first American to orbit the earth.

## June 11–15, 1962
The Port Huron Statement is issued by Students for a Democratic Society (SDS).

## October 22– November 2, 1962
The discovery of Soviet missiles in Cuba brings the world to the brink of nuclear war; the Cuban missile crisis is defused when the Soviet Union withdraws its missiles in the face of a U.S. naval blockade.

## December 31, 1962
The number of U.S. military personnel in South Vietnam reaches eleven thousand.

## February 19, 1963
Betty Friedan's *The Feminine Mystique* is published.

## April/May 1963
Civil rights demonstrators led by Martin Luther King Jr. are attacked with fire hoses and police dogs in Birmingham, Alabama.

## June 10, 1963
Kennedy signs into law the Equal Pay Act, making it illegal to set different pay scales for men and women who perform the same job.

## August 5, 1963
A nuclear test-ban treaty is signed by the United States, the Soviet Union, and Great Britain.

## August 28, 1963
The March on Washington draws over 250,000 civil rights activists to the nation's capital.

**September 15, 1963**
Four black girls are killed in a church bombing in Birmingham, Alabama.

**November 1, 1963**
President Ngo Dinh Diem of South Vietnam is overthrown in a military coup with the acquiescence of the American government; he is later assassinated.

**November 22, 1963**
President John Kennedy is assassinated in Dallas, Texas; Vice President Lyndon Johnson assumes office; captured alleged assassin Lee Harvey Oswald is murdered two days later by Jack Ruby.

**January 8, 1964**
President Lyndon B. Johnson declares an "unconditional war on poverty" in his State of the Union address.

**January 23, 1964**
The Twenty-fourth Amendment to the Constitution, which out-laws the poll tax in federal elections, is ratified.

**February 1964**
The Beatles arrive in the United States for their first American tour.

**May 22, 1964**
In a commencement address at the University of Michigan, President Johnson calls on the United States to create a "Great Society."

**June 21, 1964**
Civil rights workers James Chaney, Michael Schwerner, and Andrew Goodman disappear from Philadelphia, Mississippi; six weeks later their bodies are discovered in an earthen dam by FBI agents.

**July 2, 1964**
President Johnson signs the Civil Rights Act of 1964, prohibiting discrimination in employment and places of public accommodation.

**August 10, 1964**
The Gulf of Tonkin Resolution is passed by Congress, authorizing military action against North Vietnam in response to purported attacks on U.S. ships off the Vietnamese coast.

**August 20, 1964**
President Johnson signs the Economic Opportunity Act, which calls for the "maximum feasible participation of the poor" in antipoverty programs.

**September–December 1964**
The Free Speech Movement: Students at the University of California at Berkeley protest after university administrators try to limit political activities on the campus; 796 arrests are made on December 3.

**September 27, 1964**
The Warren Commission concludes that Lee Harvey Oswald, acting alone, killed President Kennedy.

**November 3, 1964**
Johnson overwhelmingly defeats Senator Barry Goldwater to win a full presidential term.

**February 7, 1965**
President Johnson orders bombing raids on North Vietnam.

**February 21, 1965**
Black leader Malcolm X is assassinated.

**March 21–25, 1965**
Martin Luther King Jr. leads a voting-rights march from Selma to Montgomery, Alabama.

**April 17, 1965**
The first major demonstration against the Vietnam War takes place in Washington, D.C.

**April 28, 1965**
President Johnson sends U.S. Marines to the Dominican Republic to prevent a communist takeover.

**July 25, 1965**
Acclaimed folk singer Bob Dylan breaks cultural barriers by performing with a rock band at the Newport Folk Festival.

**July 30, 1965**
President Johnson signs the Medicare bill into law.

**August 6, 1965**
President Johnson signs the Voting Rights Act of 1965.

**August 11–16, 1965**
Race riots in the black ghetto of Watts in Los Angeles leave thirty-four dead and more than one thousand injured.

**October 1965**
Cesar Chavez of the United Farm Workers Union organizes a national boycott of grapes in support of striking farmworkers.

**October 3, 1965**
The Immigration Reform Act eliminates many immigration restrictions.

**November 27, 1965**
Novelist Ken Kesey, author of *One Flew over the Cuckoo's Nest*, and a band of his followers known as the "Merry Pranksters" distribute LSD at the first "acid test" open to the public.

**January 1966**
Automatic student deferments from the draft are abolished.

**June 1966**
"Black Power" becomes the popular slogan of young black civil rights activists during a civil rights march in Mississippi.

**June 13, 1966**
In *Miranda v. Arizona* the Supreme Court declares that authorities must inform a criminal suspect of his or her constitutional rights at the time of arrest.

**July 1966**
Urban riots strike Chicago, Brooklyn, and Cleveland.

**October 1966**
The National Organization for Women (NOW) is founded.

**November 8, 1966**
Ronald Reagan wins his first race for public office when he is elected governor of California.

**January 14, 1967**
A San Francisco Be-In draws national attention to the hippie scene.

**June 1967**
The Beatles release their most influential album, *Sergeant Pepper's Lonely Hearts Club Band*.

**June 16–18, 1967**
The Monterey Pop Festival popularizes countercultural rock music and marks the beginning of the "Summer of Love."

**July 1967**
The American troop commitment to the war in Vietnam reaches 400,000.

**July 23, 1967**
Race riots in Detroit, Michigan, and Newark, New Jersey, leave 693 dead.

**October 21, 1967**
National "Stop the Draft Week" climaxes with a march on the Pentagon by fifty thousand antiwar protesters.

**November 9, 1967**
The first issue of *Rolling Stone* is published.

**1968**
The American Indian Movement (AIM) is founded in Minneapolis.

**January 1968**
The first all-female antiwar demonstration, organized by the Jeannette Rankin Brigade and the Women's Strike for Peace, is held in Washington, D.C.

**January 30, 1968**
The Tet Offensive by North Vietnamese and Viet Cong forces stuns the American military leadership and shakes the American public's confidence in America's mission in Vietnam.

**February 8, 1968**
*Soul on Ice* by Eldridge Cleaver is published.

**March 1, 1968**
The Kerner Commission on Civil Disorders publishes its report on the causes of the riots of 1967; it declares that the country is becoming "two societies—one white, one black—separate and unequal."

**March 12, 1968**
Senator Eugene McCarthy, an antiwar candidate, surprises many by finishing a strong second in the New Hampshire primary with 42 percent of the vote.

**March 16, 1968**
Senator Robert Kennedy joins the race for the Democratic presidential nomination.

In the My Lai massacre in Vietnam, U.S. troops indiscriminately kill innocent Vietnamese villagers.

**March 31, 1968**
President Johnson announces he will not seek reelection as president.

**April 4, 1968**
Martin Luther King Jr. is assassinated by James Earl Ray in Memphis, Tennessee.

**April 23–30, 1968**
Student radicals at Columbia University take over campus buildings.

**May 1968**
Peace talks to end the war in Vietnam begin in Paris.

**June 5, 1968**
Senator Robert Kennedy is assassinated hours after winning the California primary.

**August, 1968**
Feminists protest the Miss America Pageant at Atlantic City, New Jersey.

**August 25–28, 1968**
Hubert H. Humphrey is nominated for president at the Democratic National Convention in Chicago; antiwar demonstrators in a nearby park are beaten by local police.

**November 5, 1968**
Republican candidate Richard Nixon defeats Humphrey for the presidency; American Party candidate George Wallace finishes a distant third.

**January 1969**
U.S. troop strength in Vietnam reaches a peak of 543,000.

**March 1969**
The United States begins a secret bombing campaign in Cambodia.

**June 18–23, 1969**
SDS holds its last national convention and breaks into factions.

**June 27, 1969**
A riot outside the Stonewall Bar in Greenwich Village in New York City signals the start of a militant gay liberation movement.

**July 21, 1969**
Neil Armstrong becomes the first human to set foot on the moon.

**August 15–17, 1969**
The Woodstock Music and Arts Festival in White Lake, New York, draws several hundred thousand people.

**September 24, 1969**
The "Chicago 8" conspiracy trial begins; eight activists, including Abbie Hoffman, Tom Hayden, and Bobby Seale, are accused of inciting violence during the 1968 Democratic Convention.

**October 8–11, 1969**
The Weathermen, a splinter faction of SDS, hold four violent "Days of Rage" in Chicago.

**November 1969**
The American public learns of the 1968 My Lai massacre.

**December 1, 1969**
The first draft lottery of the decade is held.

# FOR FURTHER READING

Judith and Stewart Albert, *The Sixties Papers: Documents of a Rebellious Decade.* New York: Praeger, 1984. An anthology of writing from the sixties.

Elaine Brown, *A Taste of Power: A Black Woman's Story.* New York: Doubleday, 1992. The autobiography of a Black Panther member.

Peter Collier and David Horowitz, *Destructive Generation: Second Thoughts About the Sixties.* New York: Summit Books, 1989. An account of the sixties by two former left-wing activists who are now political conservatives.

Charles De Benedetti, *An American Ordeal: The Anti-War Movement of the Vietnam Era.* Syracuse, NY: Syracuse University Press, 1990. A sympathetic account of the American peace movement during the Vietnam War.

William Dudley, ed., *Opposing Viewpoints: The Civil Rights Movement.* San Diego: Greenhaven Press, 1996. An anthology of primary documents from the civil rights movement, arranged in a pro/con format.

Sara Evans, *Personal Politics: The Roots of Women's Liberation in the Civil Rights Movement and the New Left.* New York: Knopf, 1979. Evans argues that the feminist movement arose out of women's frustration with the male-dominated civil rights and student movements.

David Farber, *The Age of Great Dreams: America in the 1960s.* New York: Hill & Wang, 1994. A comprehensive overview of the decade.

Doris Kearns Goodwin, *Lyndon Johnson and the American Dream.* New York: Harper & Row, 1969. A personal account of the last years of the Johnson presidency.

Alex Haley and Malcolm X, *The Autobiography of Malcolm X.* New York: Grove Press, 1964. The controversial autobiography (cowritten by Haley, author of *Roots*) of Malcolm X, the famous black speaker and Muslim leader.

Tom Hayden, *Reunion: A Memoir.* New York: Random House, 1988. The autobiography of one of the leaders of the Students for a Democratic Society.

Gini Holland, *The 1960s: A Cultural History of the United States Through the Decades.* San Diego: Lucent Books, 1999. A basic but thorough overview of the sixties' major events.

James Miller, *"Democracy in the Streets": From Port Huron to the Siege of Chicago.* New York: Simon & Schuster, 1987. A history of the Students for a Democratic Society.

Abe Peck, *Uncovering the Sixties: The Life and Times of the Underground Press.* New York: Pantheon, 1983. A survey of the radical underground newspapers of the decade.

Daniel Simon, ed., *The Best of Abbie Hoffman*. New York: Four Walls Eight Windows, 1989. A compilation of the writings of the famous Yippie activist.

Jay Stevens, *Storming Heaven: LSD and the American Dream*. New York: Atlantic Monthly Press, 1987. A study of LSD's role in the sixties counterculture.

David P. Szatmary, *Rockin' in Time: A Social History of Rock and Roll*. An overview of the relationship between rock music and American culture.

Jules Witcover, *The Year the Dream Died: Revisiting 1968 in America*. New York: Warner Books, 1997. A history of the most turbulent year of the decade.

Leonard Wolf, ed., *Voices from the Love Generation*. Boston: Little, Brown, 1968. A collection of interviews with the hippies of Haight-Ashbury.

# WORKS CONSULTED

## Books

Terry H. Anderson, *The Movement and the Sixties*. New York: Oxford University Press, 1995. A history of sixties activism that explores the causes and effects of pivotal incidents.

Sylvan Barnet and Hugo Bedau, eds., *Critical Thinking, Reading, and Writing: A Brief Guide to Argument*. 3rd Ed. New York: St. Martin's Press, 1999. An instructional text on how to write and analyze an argument; includes examples of persuasive writing, including the text of Martin Luther King's "Letter from a Birmingham Jail."

Alexander Bloom and Wini Breines, eds., *"Takin' It to the Streets": A Sixties Reader*. New York: Oxford University Press, 1995. An anthology of documents about sixties activism, including the civil rights, women's liberation, student, and gay rights movements.

William Dudley, ed., *The 1960s: Opposing Viewpoints*. San Diego: Greenhaven Press, 1997. An extremely useful collection of primary documents, arranged in a format that highlights the conflicting views of the decade.

Alice Echols, *Daring to Be Bad: Radical Feminism in America, 1967–1975*. Minneapolis: University of Minnesota Press, 1989. A history of radical feminism in America, placed in the context of other social movements.

Michael Ferber and Staughton Lynd, *The Resistance*. Boston: Beacon Press, 1971. An account of the Resistance, a group of men who resisted the draft by illegal means to demonstrate their opposition to the Vietnam War.

Betty Friedan, *The Feminine Mystique*. New York: W. W. Norton, 1963. Considered to be the impetus of the women's liberation movement, this book revealed the dissatisfaction that many American women felt with their roles as wives and mothers.

Marvin E. Gettleman, Jane Franklin, Marilyn Young, and H. Bruce Franklin, eds., *Vietnam and America: A Documented History*. New York: Grove Press, 1985. A comprehensive collection of documents pertaining to the Vietnam War and its origins, including everything from private presidential memos to antiwar speeches.

Todd Gitlin, *The Sixties: Years of Hope, Days of Rage*. New York: Bantam Books, 1987. An intimate and colorful history of the pivotal events of the decade, written by a leader of the student movement.

Peter B. Levy, ed., *Let Freedom Ring: A Documentary History of the Modern Civil Rights Movement*. New York: Praeger, 1992. A thorough compilation of reports, speeches, and memoirs of the civil rights movement.

Malcolm X, *By Any Means Necessary*. New York: Pathfinder, 1992. A collection of speeches by and interviews with Malcolm X, in which he discusses his views on the civil rights movement, black nationalism, and the Muslim religion.

Timothy Miller, *The Hippies and American Values.* Knoxville: University of Tennessee Press, 1991. A complete analysis of the hippie movement's activities and ideals; includes many quotations from participants in the movement.

Miriam Schneir, ed., *Feminism in Our Time: The Essential Writings, World War II to the Present.* New York: Vintage Books, 1994. An intriguing anthology of speeches, articles, and essays written by a diverse range of American feminists.

**Periodicals and On-line Sources**

George A. Akerloff and Janet A. Yellen, "New Mothers, Not Married: Technology Shock, the Demise of the Shotgun Marriage, and the Increase in Out-of-Wedlock Births," *Brookings Review,* Fall 1996.

Jonathan Alter, "In the Time of Tolerance," *Newsweek,* March 30, 1998.

Dick Armey, "Public Welfare in America," *Journal of Social, Political & Economic Studies,* Summer 1994.

The Black Panther Platform, 1966. http://lists.village.virginia.edu/sixties/ HTML_docs/Resources/Primary/Manifestos/Panther_platform.html.

*Center on Budget and Policy Priorities,* "Government Benefit Programs Cut Poverty Nearly in Half Last Year, Setting a Record for Poverty Reduction," October 9, 1996. www.cbpp.org/prsfnt.htm.

Karen Davis, "Medicare Budgetary Savings: Implications for Beneficiaries," statement before the U.S. House of Representatives Committee on Ways and Means hearing on Medicare, September 22, 1995. http://epn.org/ library/ cotest.html.

Linda Ellerbee, "The Sexual Revolution: Well, It Seemed Like a Good Idea at the Time. . .," *New Choices,* April 8, 1998.

Jean Bethke Elshtain, "The Family in Trouble: Why We Should Worry," *National Forum,* Winter 1995.

Elizabeth Fox-Genovese, "The National Prospect," *Commentary,* November 1995.

William R. Garrett, "Cultural Revolution and Character Formation," *World & I,* May 1998.

*GIs United Against the War in Vietnam: Statement of Aims.* The Sixties Project. http://lists.village.virgina.edu/sixties/HTML_ docs/Resources/Primary/Manifestos/GIs_United_aims.html.

Justice John Harlan, dissenting opinion in *Plessy v. Ferguson,* 1896. www.geocities.com/CapitolHill/8569/plessy.v.ferguson.html.

Lyndon B. Johnson, "Great Society Speech," 1964, *Public Papers of the*

*Presidents of the United States, Book I (1963–64).*
http://hs1.hst.msu.edu/~hst306/documents/great.html.

Lyndon B. Johnson, "To Fulfill These Rights."
http://userwww.sfsu.edu/~mmartin/sunsh.htm.

Steve Kangas, "Myth: Welfare Increases Poverty." www.scruz.net/~kangaroo/L-welfarepoverty.htm.

Morton A. Kaplan, "The Misbegotten Sixties," *World & I*, May 1998.

John F. Kennedy, *Radio and Television Report to the American People*, June 11, 1963. www.cs.umb.edu/jfklibrary/jo61163.htm.

Martin Luther King Jr., "I Have a Dream," August 28, 1963. http://web66.coled.umn.edu/new/MLK/MLK.html.

Dean Koontz, interviewed by Nick Gillespie and Lisa Snell, "Contemplating Evil," *Reason*, November 1996.

Timothy Leary, League for Spiritual Discovery mission statement, 1967. http://leary.com/archives/text/Archives/Millbrook/Church of LSD.html.

John C. Liu and Robert E. Moffit, "A Taxpayer's Guide to the Medicare Crisis," *The Heritage Foundation Talking Points No. 10*, September 27, 1995. www.heritage.org/library/categories/healthwel/tp10.html.

Myron Magnet, "The National Prospect," *Commentary*, November 1995.

David O. McKay, "On Motherhood," 1936. www.xmission.com/~dkenison/lds/gtp/arc/dom_moth.html.

*National Organization for Women Statement of Purpose*, 1966. http://history.hanover.edu/courses/excerpts/111now.html.

Jim Powell, "A Passionate Moral Attack on Government Intervention," *Laissez Faire Books*, April 1996. http://laissezfaire.org/py6996.html.

Roger Scruton, "The Sex Files," *National Review*, October 12, 1998.

Paul W. Shaffer, "Draft Resistance in the Vietnam Era: Number of Draft Resisters." www.saas.upenn.edu/~pws/60s/numbers.html.

Valerie Solanas, "The SCUM Manifesto," Phoenix Press, 1968. www.ai.mit.edu/~shivers/rants/scum.html.

U.S. State Department, *Aggression from the North: The Record of North Vietnam's Campaign to Conquer South Vietnam*, February 27, 1965. http://wiretap.spies.com/ftp.items/Gov/us-History/Vietnam/whitepaper.txt.

Kenneth Whyte, "Allan Rock," *Saturday Night*, November 1995.

William R. Wineke, "Slip on Those Rose-Colored Glasses for Just a Moment," *Wisconsin State Journal*, April 25, 1998.

# INDEX

## ABOUT THE AUTHOR

Jennifer Hurley works as a series editor for Greenhaven Press, teaches composition at the University of Phoenix, and writes short fiction. She attended graduate school at Boston University, where she received an M.A. in creative writing, and currently resides in San Diego with her cat, Emma.